THE HORSE·LOVER'S DIARY

This diary belongs to

Name

Address

Telephone

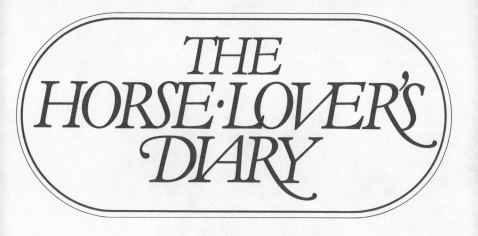

THE HORSE·LOVER'S DIARY

by **Christilot Hanson Boylen**
with Shelley Tanaka

Illustrated by Elaine Macpherson

Introduced by Walter Farley

A Random House 🏠 Madison Press Book
New York

Published simultaneously in Canada by
McClelland and Stewart Limited

ISBN 0-394-86104-3

Produced by
Madison Press Books
149 Lowther Avenue
Toronto, Ontario
Canada M5R 3M5

Design: René Demers
Front cover photograph: © Elisabeth Weiland
Editor: Shelley Tanaka

Because this page cannot legibly
accommodate all acknowledgments
to reproduce previously published
material, they appear on page 175.

Manufactured in the United States of America

Introduction

I have been writing the Black Stallion books and other horse stories for over thirty years. If it has not made me a professional horseman, I feel justified in thinking that I am a professional observer of horsemen and horsewomen engaged in the business of training horses for fun or profit.

My research for story material has taken me to all areas, here and abroad, where people work with horses–from 4-H and pony clubs to major racetracks, from show rings to circus rings, from *haute école* to open jumping, from competitive dressage to eventing–all breeds, all kinds of people, and usually with the same objective in mind: the ultimate performance of the horse to the best of its capabilities.

However, despite all this experience, I realize that what I believed as a child, I believe now. It is possible–in fact necessary–to regard your horse not as a working machine whose only true love is the feed you give him but as a close friend to be loved. People who "put down" such love and honest sentiment between horse and rider are usually without feelings and sensitivity themselves. It has been proved countless times at the racetrack, show ring and barnyard. Call it what you like–love, friendship, compatibility–but there is a *union* between horse and rider that is understood by each.

This union, however, works between rider and mount only when combined with the rider's hard work, patience, perseverance, kindness, tact and, of course, experience, however you get it. And if you truly care for your horse and develop an understanding with him, you will not only have a friend but will acquire greater courage, confidence and awareness of yourself.

My friend Chris Boylen is well acquainted with all this, for she is one of the finest dressage riders and trainers I know. I hope that some of her magic, the almost mystical gift that she has with horses, will find its way to you.

Walter Farley
Venice, Florida

The Horse-Lover's Diary

I have always loved all animals, but horses are my passion. Even at the age of five my favorite games involved "playing horse"– running and jumping obstacles that I had built from brooms and boxes.

Since no one in my family had ever had any contact with horses, my parents desperately hoped that I would soon outgrow my "horsey phase." They wanted me to turn my attention to drama and piano lessons instead.

I enjoyed music, but, like most kids, I hated practicing. In fact, I was so negligent that my father decided to offer me the ultimate incentive. He told me he would let me start riding lessons if I passed my piano exams with honors two years in a row!

The transformation was miraculous. I practiced diligently, always dreaming about riding a horse of my very own, and I passed my tests with flying colors.

The drama lessons also paid off. When I was nine, I auditioned for a role in a national television production and landed a regular part. The money I earned was kept in my "horse" account, and when I turned ten, with all my piano obligations fulfilled, my parents allowed me to join the Toronto and North York Pony Club, and the search for my first horse began.

From that day I ate, slept and lived horses. I used to love even the smell of the tack–cleaned, oiled and shined to an old burnished shimmer. I learned everything I could about grooming, bandaging and first aid, and read every horse book I could get my hands on. I was lucky to have spent those early years in the pony club system where basic good horsemanship is stressed, as well as the disciplines of dressage, cross-country and stadium jumping.

When I turned fourteen my parents were able to send me and my horse, Bonheur, to Germany for one year, to study dressage with a former Olympic gold medalist. Those eleven months may have been the most important of my life in shaping my ideas and work habits. In Germany I had to learn a strange language and cope with being away from my parents and friends. I also learned quickly that in the international equestrian world, the responsibility for my success or failure rested entirely on my own shoulders.

It was a lonely, exhausting and grueling year, but on my return to Canada, the experience Bonheur and I had gained immediately began to show results. We were virtually unbeatable in the junior dressage division, and we took our fair share of the open classes as well. Eventually, with a lot of hard work, superb coaching and the commitment and support of my parents, we made it to Grand Prix standard and the 1964 Tokyo Olympics! At seventeen, I was the youngest person ever to have competed in the Grand Prix de Dressage event at an Olympic Games.

Since 1964 I have competed in many international equestrian competitions. My most promising horse at the moment is a Canadian-bred horse called Dior. We placed seventh in the World Dressage Championships in Lausanne, Switzerland, in the Prix St. Georges, and I hope we will make the Olympics in Los Angeles in 1984.

In the last few years I have been involved in setting up an equestrian centre outside Toronto. The International Equestrian Sports Centre has facilities for equestrian training and provides a site for major competitions. Through my work at the Centre and the many clinics that I have given across North America, I've had the opportunity to help train a number of young riders.

I know I am extremely fortunate that my work involves something I love to do. Riding has brought me a great share of happiness, some sadness, as well as a lot of aches and pains. But today, every time I ride through the bush behind my house or watch my pupils train at the Centre, I get a warm, satisfied feeling about having fulfilled what was once just a fantastic dream. I hope that everyone who loves horses will be lucky enough to experience the unique challenge that this wonderful sport can bring.

Christilot Hanson Boylen
International Equestrian Sports Centre
Toronto, 1983

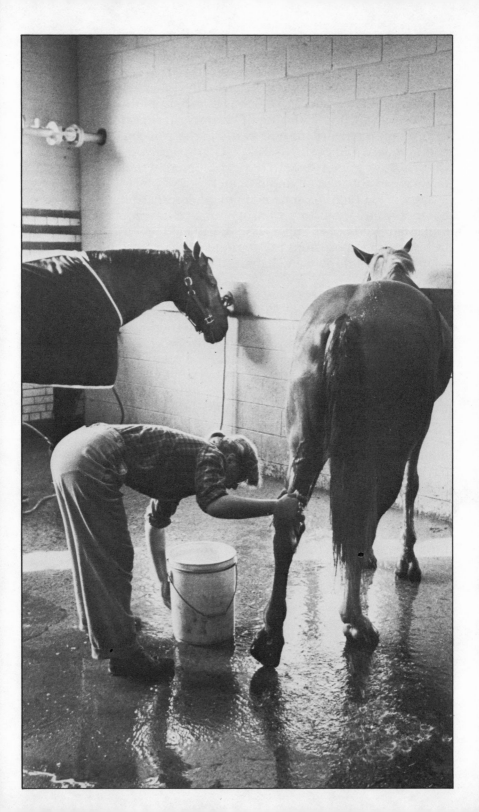

Things to do in
JANUARY 19___

Date	16
1	17
2	18
3	19
4	20
5	21
6	22
7	23
8	24
9	25
10	26
11	27
12	28
13	29
14	30
15	31

It is the common law of horsedom that when a mare drops a foal the yearling running at her side must be banished. One is enough for her to nurse and care for. The stallion sees to it and drives them away. At first they try desperately to get back and the struggle continues for days. They cannot conceive of life, separated from their dams. Eventually, bitten and bleeding and scarred, they accept their first serious defeat and stand at a distance in woebegone postures with heads hanging, eyes turned wistfully back towards the herd. But soon comes consolation, for they band together in their affliction. Often permanent attachments are formed. They learn a new and independent way of life, find their own food and shelter and glorious fun begins.

Mary O'Hara, *The Green Grass of Wyoming*

JANUARY

The earliest ancestor of the horse was *Eohippus*, or the dawn horse, an animal about 12 inches high who lived 55 to 40 million years ago. This animal lived in swampy forests and browsed on leaves, rather than grazing on grass. Its feet were soft and it ran on tiptoe in a choppy, up-and-down gait. The modern horse still walks on just the tip of the third toe, which is greatly strengthened by a tough hoof. This highly specialized hoof can move at very high speeds on hard ground.

Straight away, all in front of the wind, and scattering clouds around her, all I knew of the speed we made was the frightful flash of her shoulders, and her mane like trees in a tempest. I felt the earth under us rushing away, and the air left far behind us . . .

R.D. Blackmore,
Lorna Doone

JANUARY

Horses are measured in hands, from the ground to the top of the withers.
One hand equals four inches. A horse that is described as being 15.2 hh
(hands high), for example, is 15 hands and 2 inches high – 62 inches in all.

POINTS OF A HORSE

1 forehead

2 forelock

3 muzzle

4 jaw bars

5 cheek

6 throttle

7 neck

8 shoulder

9 chest

10 forearm

11 knee

12 fetlock

13 ergot

14 cannon

15 chestnut

16 elbow

17 belly

18 barrel or rib cage

19 sheath

20 gaskin

21 pastern

22 coronet

23 hoof

24 heel

25 hock

26 tail

27 quarters

28 dock

29 croup

30 flank

31 loins

32 back

33 withers

34 mane

35 crest

36 poll

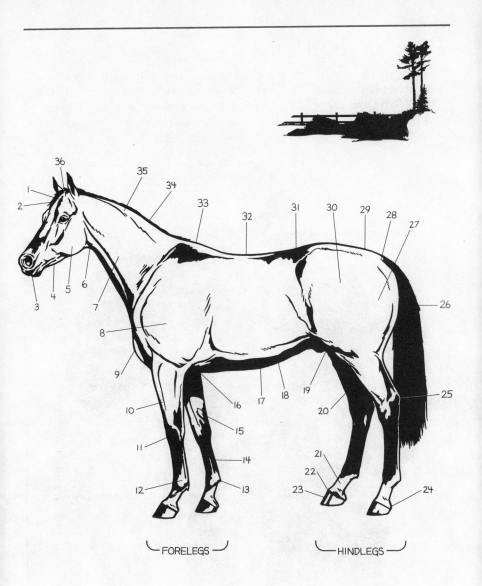

FORELEGS HINDLEGS

Rider of the Month

Cindy Ishoy learned to ride as a child in Germany. When she was 19 she competed as a dressage rider in the Pan-American Games and went on to ride on two Olympic teams. "I'm really competitive," she says. "I've always driven myself...because I don't think I'm overly talented. I have to work really hard to stay fit. It's a challenge."

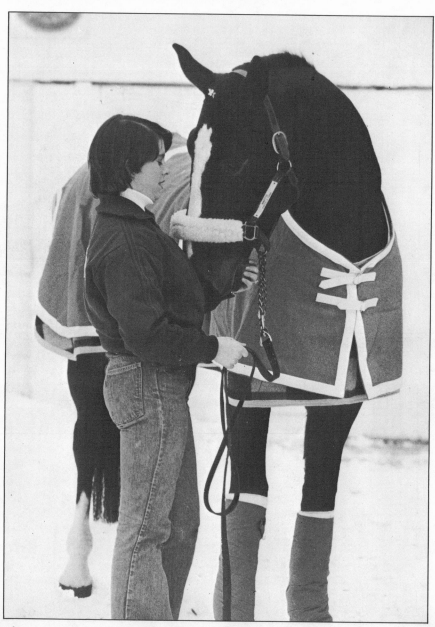

JANUARY

A horse's chestnuts (also called night eyes) are vestigial toes. No two
chestnuts are alike – they are as individual as fingerprints.

O! for a horse with wings!

William Shakespeare, *Cymbeline*

JANUARY

Most horses weigh between 900 and 1,400 pounds, although some draft horses weigh over one ton.

Things to do in
FEBRUARY 19___

Date	16
1	17
2	18
3	19
4	20
5	21
6	22
7	23
8	24
9	25
10	26
11	27
12	28
13	29
14	
15	

Andy closed in to Minette's head, shortening the near rein lest she buck, bolt, rear or otherwise express disapproval. Colin stood by . . . with one hand extended under Jane's raised foot as he had seen it on the films. With a mild feeling of anti-climax, Jane found herself seated in perfect comfort on Minette's back. Minette, throughout the performance, had gazed impersonally out to sea, as though unaware of any unusual activity behind her ears.

After a few minutes of unrhythmic, stomach-jolting, lurching and clutching at Minette's hogged neck, Jane decided she could manage. Minette, narrow-withered, provided her with an easy grip. . . . She relaxed her tense muscles, as it became apparent Minette did not intend to bolt home, sat up straight with the small of her back pulled in, and tucked her elbows in to her sides. She turned her knees in, and let the snaffle slide easily between the third and fourth fingers until it was the length she wanted. Minette jogged happily along. She had a pleasant gait and a surprisingly light mouth. In fact–after quarter of an hour Jane cautiously reviewed the prospects–riding the milkcart horse was quite an enjoyable experience.

Mary Treadgold, *No Ponies* (illustrated by Ruth Gervis)

FEBRUARY

When you are sitting on a horse, the left side is called the horse's near side. The right side is the horse's off side. Horses should always be mounted and dismounted on the near side.

To Jeff he was like a leaping flame. He was thundering hooves shattering the silence of a moonlight night. He was a breath-catching glimpse of speed and plunging power in a blinding flash of rain-streaked lightning.

Walt Morey, *Runaway Stallion*

FEBRUARY

A horse uses its sense of smell to become familiar with things, and horses will often want to sniff at unfamiliar objects, such as jumping obstacles, a new saddle or strange people. The Gypsies believe that the best way to make friends with a horse is to blow gently on its nostrils.

HORSE & PONY BREEDS

Although there are over 200 different breeds of horses in the world today, most breeds fall into four main categories: harness horses, saddle horses, draft horses and ponies.

Harness

Harness horses were originally developed as driving horses, to pull carriages and coaches. They are also used in trotting and harness racing.

Cleveland Bay
This breed from Yorkshire, England, was a popular carriage horse at one time, but today it is often mated with a Thoroughbred to produce a hunting and jumping horse. It is surefooted, but not exceptionally fast, and is always bay-colored, without any markings.

Friesian
Originally from Friesland in the Netherlands, this black harness horse was bred in the Middle Ages to carry knights in armor. It is distinguished by its thick, curly mane and tail.

Gelderland
A horse from the Netherlands with a wide body and high tail. Originally a farm horse, the Gelderland, crossed with a Thoroughbred, makes a very good riding horse.

Hackney
A high-stepping English harness and trotting horse that is a cross between a Thoroughbred stallion and a Norfolk Trotter mare (an English draft breed). Its high, bushy tail is often docked, and it can be easily distinguished by its exaggerated but graceful step.

Standardbred
A famous American harness-racing horse whose name dates from 1879, when the registered trotting horse had to be able to reach a standard speed. The Standardbred is primarily used for racing.

Saddle

Saddle horses are horses used for riding—racing, showing, polo, dressage or recreational riding.

American Saddlebred
In pioneer days this horse was used as a plantation harness horse, but it is now a popular show horse. It has a proud carriage and is often called "the peacock of the horse world." The Saddlebred has three to five ambling gaits, carries its tail high and has high knee action.

Appaloosa
Originally developed by the Nez Percé Indians of the American northwest, this horse is easily recognized by its flashy appearance and exotic coloring. The horse is born dark, but whitens with age, and spots appear that usually cluster over the rump. The Appaloosa is used as a Western horse and is often chosen to perform in circuses.

Arab
The elegant Arab is the oldest purebred in the world and is often used to improve other breeds. The head is small and delicate, with a concave ("dish-faced") profile, and its muzzle is so small that it is said that this horse can drink from a teacup. The Arab is a great long-distance competition horse.

Lipizzaner
A famous show breed that originated in Austria in 1564 and is used in the Spanish Riding School of Vienna. This athletic and intelligent horse is born black, but turns almost white by the time it is ten years old. The Lipizzaner is an excellent horse for high-level dressage movements.

Quarter Horse
Originally bred in Virginia as a racehorse for quarter-mile tracks, this horse is one of the most popular American breeds, often used for Western riding and as a ranch horse. It is also an intelligent all-round workhorse. In recent years the Quarter horse has been crossed with the Thoroughbred, making it faster than ever.

Thoroughbred
Bred for the racetrack, this athletic horse is a descendant of the Arab. It has a long, smooth stride and is powerful and elegant. With its long legs, it is noted for its speed—a Thoroughbred can run 40 mph for a short distance. The Thoroughbred is often used in the hunt and as a show horse. It can become an excellent jumper and dressage horse, but may be quick-tempered and excitable.

Warmblood
A Warmblood is a horse bred specifically for competition in one of the three Olympic disciplines, i.e., jumping, dressage, three-day event. It is usually a half-bred horse that is then crossed with a Thoroughbred.

Draft

Draft horses are bred for heavy labor, to work on farms and to pull heavy loads. With the exception of elephants, they are the world's strongest animals.

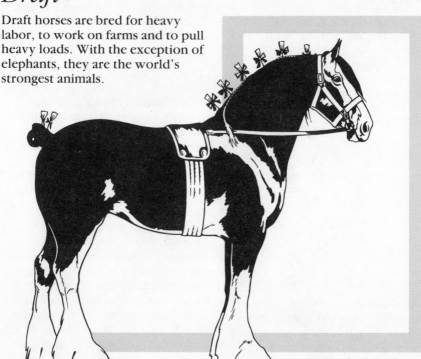

Clydesdale

A Scottish draft horse that is strong but very active and is not as heavy or large as other draft breeds. Its feet are big and rounded with shaggy coverings of hair or feather around the fetlocks. The face, feet and belly are often white. A very talented jumper or dressage horse can be produced when a Clydesdale is crossed with a Thoroughbred.

Percheron

A popular draft breed from northern France, this horse is noted for its tremendous strength, easy handling and dependability. The colt is born black but becomes dappled gray with age. This enormous horse can weigh over one ton and is often used in circuses.

Shire

The tallest horse in the world. Often reaching a height of 18 hands (72 inches), the Shire is an enormous draft breed that was once used to carry knights in armor. The Shire is hardworking and powerful with a slow-moving, shuffling gait.

Ponies

Ponies are distinct breeds of small horses that are usually no higher than 14.2 hands (58 inches). Most ponies are strong, intelligent and hardy, with compact bodies and short, sturdy legs. They are often used as work animals and as riding animals for children.

Camargue
An ancient pony breed descended from the Arab. The Camargue is one of the few wild breeds to run free in southern France.

Exmoor
The Exmoor still runs wild in southwest England, and is the oldest breed in England. It is hardy, powerful and strong-willed, with a smooth, flat trot. The Exmoor pony is brown, with a light-colored muzzle and belly.

Fjord
A good-natured driving and work pony that is native to Norway. The Fjord pony is easy to identify by the black hairs in its mane and tail. The mane is often cut in a crest shape.

Haflinger
A hardy, palomino-colored breed from the Tyrol mountains in Austria, this surefooted pony is often used as a pack and draft animal. It has a heavy head, flaxen mane and tail, and usually lives to a great age.

New Forest
The New Forest pony from southern England is one of the larger pony breeds, standing between 12 and 14 hands (48 to 56 inches). It is a reliable riding animal and has a reputation for being quiet.

Pony of the Americas
A recent American breed developed in 1956 from the Appaloosa, Quarter horse and Arab, this pony has spotted coloring, often with a dark muzzle. Like its Arab ancestors, it has a dish-faced profile, large, wide-set eyes and small ears.

Shetland
Once used to carry peat, this well-known pony is originally from the rocky Shetland Islands north of Scotland. The Shetland has a stout body and a short, strong neck. It is very hardy for its size and can make a good riding pony for small children.

Welsh Mountain
This pony, with its flowing mane and tail, is considered by many to be the most beautiful of the pony breeds. It has Arab and Thoroughbred blood and makes a good riding and show pony. The Welsh Mountain has a delicate head, fine coat and graceful limbs.

To keep track of the different horse and pony breeds that you see, use the checklist on pages 162 and 163.

Rider of the Month

George Morris began riding at the age of nine and became a member of the U.S. Equestrian Team when he was 19. He has ridden in the Olympics, Pan-American Games and Grand Prix of Aachen. He now lives in Pitts-town, New Jersey, where he operates one of the leading hunter-jumper stables in North America. He is shown riding "Brussels," a gray Dutch-bred mare.

FEBRUARY

The Przewalski (shi-VAL-skee) or Mongolian Wild Horse is the only breed that has never been tamed by man. There are only about 300 of these horses in existence – about 150 in zoos and the rest in wild herds in the Gobi Desert of Mongolia.

Thou must learn the thoughts of the noble horse
Whom thou wouldst ride.
Be not indiscreet in thy demands,
Nor require him to perform indiscreetly.

Johann Wolfgang von Goethe

FEBRUARY

Today there are about 65 million horses in the world. Most of these are saddle horses used for riding.

Things to do in
MARCH *19__*

Date		16	
1		17	
2		18	
3		19	
4		20	
5		21	
6		22	
7		23	
8		24	
9		25	
10		26	
11		27	
12		28	
13		29	
14		30	
15		31	

My horse has a hoof like striped agate;
His fetlock is like a fine eagle-plume;
His legs are like quick lightning.
My horse's body is like an eagle-plumed arrow;
My horse has a tail like a trailing black cloud.
His mane is made of short rainbows.
My horse's ears are made of round corn.
My horse's eyes are made of big stars.
My horse's teeth are made of white shell.
The long rainbow is in his mouth for a bridle,
And with it I guide him.

Paul Goble, *The Girl Who Loved Wild Horses*
(illustrated by Paul Goble)

MARCH

Except for the whale, the horse has the largest eyes of any mammal in the world.

She watched the horse's mane blowing in the breeze and felt the horse's doubts and her own working together . . .

K.M. Peyton, *Flambards in Summer*

MARCH

The Chinese first tamed the horse in 3500 B.C. Organized equitation was developed during the Greek civilization, around 400 B.C.

COLORS & MARKINGS

Colors

In domestic horses we differentiate between four basic colors: brown, chestnut, black and gray. The only truly white horse is the albino, which lacks all color except in its eyes, which are pink. Most white horses that you see are in fact gray horses that have gone white with age. When there is doubt as to the color of the coat, then the color of the points (muzzle, ears, mane, tail and hooves) is the deciding factor.

Brown or bay
A pure brown shade, running from light to dark, but always having darker legs and black mane and tail.

Chestnut or sorrel
A reddish-brown coloring of light to dark shades, but always with mane and tail of the same color or somewhat lighter than the body coat.

Black
The bodies, manes and tails are uniformly black. Any markings are white.

Gray or roan
These horses can be of any of the three basic colors but have white hairs interspersed all over the body. They grow lighter with every change of hair. A strawberry or chestnut roan has chestnut hairs sprinkled with white. A blue roan has a black or brown coat with a sprinkling of white.

Pinto or calico
Horses with blotched or spotted patterns. A piebald has large, irregular patches of black and white. A skewbald has large patches of white and brown.

Head Markings

The white markings on a horse's head are described as follows:

Star
This is a white spot between or slightly above the eyes.

Blaze
A broad white line of hair running from the forehead down the nose to the nostrils.

Snip
A small area of white around the nostrils and upper lip area.

Strip
A narrow white line running from the forehead down the nose to the nostrils.

White face or bald face
A horse with a white forehead, nose and muzzle.

STAR

BLAZE

SNIP

STRIP

BALD FACE

Leg Markings

White leg markings can range from those just on the coronet to full stockings–white on the leg from the coronet to the knee or hock.

CORONET PASTERN FETLOCK SOCK STOCKING

Rider of the Month

Torchy Millar began riding on his family's farm in Cochrane, Alberta. He entered his first pony club competition at the age of six and went on to become a member of the Canadian Equestrian Jumping Team. He has competed in the Olympics, Pan-American Games and World Cup Grand Prix events. He's shown riding ''Phoenix Park,'' a gray, Irish-bred gelding.

MARCH

Horses communicate with different sounds and movements. A snort is usually a danger signal, and a whinny means the horse is excited. When a horse lashes its tail back and forth, it may mean it is about to kick. A stamping or prancing horse is showing nervousness or excitement.

There is something about the outside of a horse that is good for the inside of a man.

Winston Churchill

MARCH

Many trainers believe that giving food rewards teaches a horse to nip.

HOME EXERCISE PROGRAM

Riding correctly demands a high level of fitness and coordination on the part of the rider as well as the horse. In addition to improving your general fitness by engaging in some form of aerobic exercise (jogging, walking, swimming, etc.), you can do the following exercises at home to improve your posture and balance and strengthen the riding muscles.

1) Lie flat on your back with knees bent and the soles of your feet flat on the floor. Stretch your arms out to the side at shoulder level. Relax. Press the small of your back into the floor. Hold this position for a few seconds, then release. Repeat ten times.

This "pelvic tilt" exercise will help you feel and strengthen the muscles that brace the back in riding.

2) Sit on a hard chair with soles of the feet flat on the floor. Keep your head up and spine perfectly straight (imagine that there is a string attached to the top of your head, pulling you straight up). Holding both arms straight out in front of you, use your thigh muscles to lift your seat forward and out of the chair. Return to the starting position. Do this exercise ten times, aiming for a smooth, controlled movement.

In addition to improving your balance, this exercise will strengthen your upper and lower leg muscles.

3) Kneel on the floor with knees and heels together. Hold your spine completely straight and hold your hands behind your neck, with elbows out to the side. Imitate a controlled "riding" or posting movement, lifting and lowering your thighs and upper body. Work your way up gradually to three minutes (you will feel considerable muscle pain in the beginning). When you have mastered this exercise, try doing it with your knees about 12 inches apart.

Learning to "post" on the ground to music will help develop your feeling for rhythm.

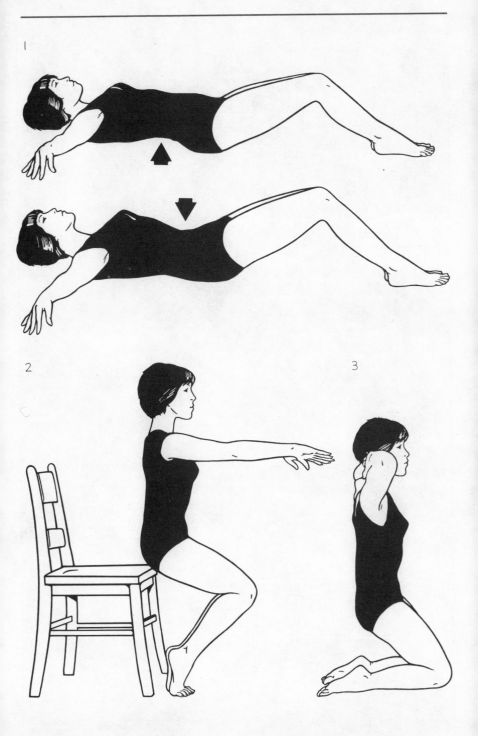

1

2

3

Things to do in
APRIL 19__

Date	16
1	17
2	18
3	19
4	20
5	21
6	22
7	23
8	24
9	25
10	26
11	27
12	28
13	29
14	30
15	

But the brute, when she had finished, did look lovely. Ruth was cheered when she went out again in the evening, and saw him grazing under the trees in the last of the sun, the golden light adding an extra burnish to the work she had put in on his coat during the afternoon. He had filled out beautifully since the spring, yet was not too fat, for Ruth had been keeping him in the garden all day, where the grass was very spare, and only letting him into the builder's field at night. And his extra inches were muscle, not flabby fat; his shoulders and quarters were hard and strong, his eyes bright with good health. When he saw her at the fence he came cantering up, as he always did now, and pushed his nose at her eagerly. She rarely gave him titbits, for he had taken to biting when she had given him too many. Now, at least, he never bit, but still gobbled his lips at her in his thrusting pony way, all bounce and push. Fly had never been a pony to just stand and let himself be stroked.

K.M. Peyton, *Fly-by-Night*
(illustrated by K.M. Peyton)

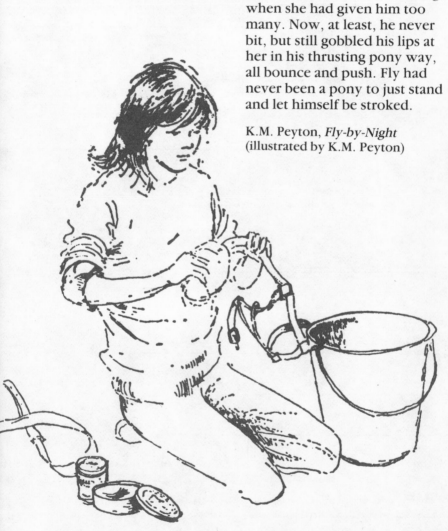

APRIL

Horses generally live to the age of 30. One year of a horse's life is said to equal about three years of a human's life. Most work and harness horses are retired in their early twenties. Racehorses are usually retired at the age of four. The Lipizzan stallions of the Spanish Riding School often perform until the age of 20.

Whenever the horse stopped (which it did very often), he fell off in front; and, whenever it went on again (which it generally did rather suddenly), he fell off behind. Otherwise he kept on pretty well, except that he had a habit of now and then falling off sideways . . .

Lewis Carroll, *Through the Looking-Glass* (illustrated by John Tenniel)

APRIL

The Puritans, who believed that it was sinful to race, defined a race as a contest between horses that were made to run as fast as possible. Since trotting was not a racing gait, trotting contests were not considered to be racing.

PACES

Horses have four principal paces–walk, trot, canter and gallop.

Walk

There are four separate hoofbeats. This is a comfortable pace for a rider, who sits in the saddle in a nearly erect position with head and feet in the same line of balance. In a good walk, the hindleg should overreach the print of the forefoot.

Trot or Jog

There are two hoofbeats and the legs move in diagonal pairs. There is a moment of suspension when all four legs are in the air. The rider may either "post" to the trot or execute a "sitting trot" by remaining in the saddle.

Canter or Lope

There are three hoofbeats–the horse bounds, leading with one foreleg. The canter requires greater weight ahead of the balance line than the walk or trot. When cantering in a circle, the inside legs should lead.

Gallop

There are four hoofbeats–the legs move quickly one after another. The gallop is an unrestrained canter, but the moment of suspension, when all four legs are off the ground, is much longer. The rider inclines the body forward, with more weight on the stirrups, to remain over the horse's centre of gravity. This is also the position used when jumping.

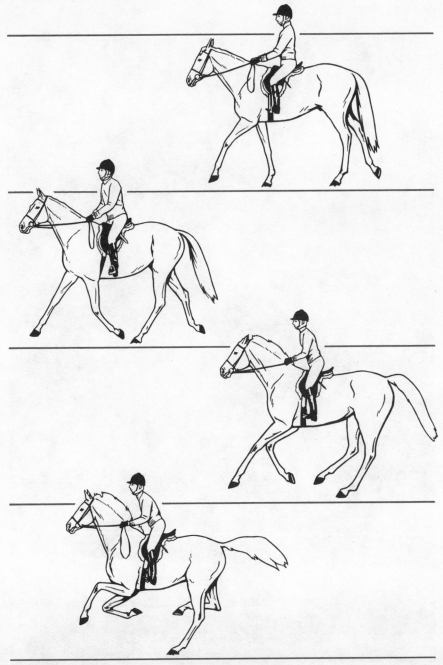

Rider of the Month

Elizabeth Ashton was born in England and began competing in international horse shows at the age of 17. She is Canada's premier three-day event competitor and is now preparing for the 1984 Olympics. She is shown riding "Sunrise."

APRIL

In the racing world, the birthdays of racehorses are always considered to be January 1st. Even though a foal is usually born between February and June, the following January 1st it is considered to be a yearling. Racehorse breeders prefer racing foals to be born as early in the year as possible.

Give a man a horse he can ride,
Give a man a boat he can sail.

James Thomson, ''Sunday up the River''

APRIL

Try to keep your horse on a regular schedule. Your horse will not understand if you sleep in and miss its morning feeding or exercise. If you do want to change your horse's feeding or exercise routine, do it gradually to allow the horse time to get used to the new pattern.

Things to do in
MAY 19___

Date	16
1	17
2	18
3	19
4	20
5	21
6	22
7	23
8	24
9	25
10	26
11	27
12	28
13	29
14	30
15	31

I had eyes for only one. The black pony in the lead. He ran like he loved being free. His head was up, sharp ears forward, black mane and tail flying in the wind. The sun made his black coat glisten like satin. The big muscles across shoulders and legs rippled like light flashes on water. They pounded past right under the rock where I crouched. I watched until they were out of sight. The whole thing took maybe two minutes.

Every Saturday since the winter weather had broken I'd climbed up here to watch that pony pass. The sight of him did something to me I've never quite been able to explain. He was more than tremendous strength and speed and beauty of motion. He set me dreaming.

Walt Morey, *Year of the Black Pony*

MAY

Unlike humans, horses have teeth that continue to grow as they wear down from use. One way to tell a horse's age is by seeing how many of the cups or hollows in the teeth have been worn away.

The one best precept–the golden rule in dealing with a horse–is never to approach him angrily. Anger is so devoid of forethought that it will often drive a man to do things which in a calmer mood he will regret.

Xenophon

MAY

In colder climates, horses that are kept indoors for many months of the year, or who are often kept covered by exercise blankets, may not have enough exposure to bright sunlight. Sunlight is needed for the manufacture of vitamin D in the skin, so vitamin D supplements may be necessary for these horses.

CHOOSING YOUR HORSE

Whether you are buying a horse of your own or just choosing one to ride regularly, you will want to pick a horse that is well built and suited to your height, weight and riding ability. A well-built horse is usually healthier, easier to train and more comfortable to ride, as well as being more attractive.

There are certain desirable physical characteristics that experts look for in a riding or show horse.

–A broad *forehead* and eyes that are set far apart contribute to an attractive head.

–Forward-pricked *ears* often indicate a happy, easygoing horse. Flattened ears, pinned against the neck, are a danger sign, usually a warning of violent action.

–Big, shining *eyes* are a sign of good health and temperament. Be suspicious of a horse that flashes its eyes nervously and looks backward frequently.

–A horse with a very long *neck* ("rubber-necked") may be difficult to control. An exceptionally short-necked horse may have a short stride and choppy gait.

–The highest point of the horse's backline, the *withers*, should be gently rounded but well defined, so that a saddle will fit properly.

–A deep and broad *chest* provides ample room for the heart and lungs, and the barrel or body should be rounded to allow lots of room for the digestive organs.

–The *cannon* should be short and straight, to take the horse's weight more effectively. Horses for show-jumping or hunting need strong, long *forearms*.

–*Pasterns* should be sloping to act as shock absorbers.

–The *hooves* should be round, thick and tough to cushion the horse's step, and the feet should be matched in shape, so that the weight is distributed evenly. Hooves should also be free of cracks.

When choosing a horse, you should consider its breed and size. Certain breeds (e.g., Quarter horse, Arab) are more suitable for Western-style and trail riding while some breeds (e.g., Thoroughbred) may be better for English-style riding. If you are unable to provide your horse with daily exercise, it's best not to choose a horse that is high in Thoroughbred blood. It may be more temperamental than Warmblood breeds.

It is better to choose a horse that is a little too big rather than too small, but the horse should not be so big that it is difficult to control.

It is also important to consider a horse's age. Generally, novice riders should choose a mature horse (between 6 and 12)–young horses need experienced riders. Never overestimate your riding ability when choosing a horse. Training a young horse requires a great deal of time, patience, experience and talent.

The main qualities to look for are willingness and intelligence. Don't mistake sluggishness for gentleness–a lively horse can also be gentle. You will also want to choose a horse whose personality is compatible with yours. Sometimes opposites attract–a quiet horse may need a more aggressive rider, while an excitable horse may be controlled more easily by a calm rider.

Remember that the perfect horse does not exist, so don't be too rigid in your demands for a certain appearance, age or breed, and don't forget to look for a horse's good points as well as its flaws.

If you are lucky enough to be looking for a horse to buy, seek the advice of professionals. A horse is an expensive purchase. Have it examined by a horse expert and a veterinarian, and ride the horse or watch it being ridden as much as possible before making a final decision.

Rider of the Month

Frank Chapot has been a member of the U.S. Equestrian Team for over 25 years and is presently coach of the team. He has competed in six Olympic Games and three Pan-American Games and has represented the United States in international competitions throughout Europe, South America, Japan, Canada and Mexico. He is Secretary of the American Horse Shows Association and is also a director of the National Horse Show held in Madison Square Garden.

MAY

All Thoroughbreds and most harness horses that have been raced have their registration numbers tattooed inside their upper lips.

Now the great winds shoreward blow,
Now the salt tides seaward flow;
Now the wild white horses play,
Champ and chafe and toss in the spray.

Matthew Arnold, "The Forsaken Merman"

MAY

Never feed a hot or tired horse. After hard work let your horse rest for at least an hour before feeding, giving it a few mouthfuls of water every quarter hour. Never allow a hot horse to drink a large amount of cold water.

Things to do in

JUNE 19__

Date		16	
1		17	
2		18	
3		19	
4		20	
5		21	
6		22	
7		23	
8		24	
9		25	
10		26	
11		27	
12		28	
13		29	
14		30	
15			

The crowd began to scream as the fighting horses came thundering toward them. Sun Raider was surging ahead. Cyclone was falling back–the Black had him! Sun Raider was two lengths in front, his jockey batting away with his whip. The Black started moving up. Now he was a length behind. No whip was being used on him–his jockey was like a small burr lost in the stallion's thick, black mane.

Hysteria swept the crowd as the horses passed them for the second time–the finish wire only one hundred yards away. "He'll never get Sun Raider!" yelled the sportscaster. The stallion flashed by the stands, going faster with every magnificent stride. With a sudden spurt he bore down on Sun Raider. For a moment he hesitated as he came alongside. The crowd gasped as the Black's ears went back and he bared his teeth. There was a movement on his back; his jockey's hand rose and fell on the stallion's side for the first time in the race. Into the lead the Black swept, past the cheering thousands–a step, a length, two lengths ahead–then the almighty giant plunged under the wire.

Walter Farley, *The Black Stallion*

JUNE

The rodeo is the classic Western sport, and it includes five standard events – calf roping, saddle-bronc riding, bareback-bronc riding, bull riding and steer wrestling. More than 1,000 rodeos are held in North America every year.

The rhythm of the ride carried them on and on, and she knew that the horse was as eager as she, as much in love with the speed and air and freedom.

Georgess McHargue, *The Horseman's Word*

JUNE

Check your riding boots periodically for ripped or loose stitches and worn heels, soles, cuffs, seams and backstraps. Have repairs done immediately. Boots that are ill-fitting or in need of repair are not safe.

TACK

The saddle, bridle and other horse equipment are called the tack.

Saddles are used to help the rider keep a balanced seat. There are two basic styles of riding–English riding and Western riding. There are two kinds of English saddles–the *forward-seat hunter/jumper saddle* and the *dressage saddle*.

The *hunter/jumper saddle* has an extended forward flap to accommodate the rider's knee position. The stirrup leathers are short. The *dressage saddle* has longer stirrups and long, straight flaps to accommodate the rider's straighter legs.

The *Western* or *stock saddle* is heavier than the English saddle and has a deep seat, high cantle and a high pommel with a horn for attaching a lariat. Western saddles are usually placed on blankets. There should be at least two inches of blanket between the saddle and the horse's back.

The *saddle pad* is used to protect the horse's back as well as the saddle during exercise. Saddle pads can be made of cloth, rubber, sheepskin or felt.

The *girth* is the strap that goes under the horse's belly and keeps the saddle in place. Girths can be made of webbing, nylon cord, leather or elastic. A girth may have to be adjusted once the horse has moved around or been ridden a bit.

The best *stirrups* are made of stainless steel. Stirrup leathers should be checked regularly for signs of wear. Heavyweight stirrups with broad treads are the easiest to keep on the foot.

The *bit* is the rubber or metal bar that goes in the horse's mouth. With the reins, it is the main means of controlling the horse. There are two basic types of bits–the snaffle and the curb bit.

The *bridle* is the horse's headgear that supports the bit. The two most common bridles are the snaffle bridle and the double bridle.

There are various kinds of *nosebands*. The *cavesson noseband* is the most straightforward type. The *dropped noseband* fastens below the bit to control the horse's tendency to open its mouth. The *flash noseband* is a combination of a dropped noseband and cavesson.

The *reins* are made of webbing or leather. Two reins are used with a double bridle. Reins should be checked frequently for signs of wear.

A *martingale* is a device used to control a horse's head carriage.

Other pieces of horse equipment are blankets, traveling and exercise bandages, tail guards, boots and hoods.

Cleaning Tack

To clean tack and prevent it from hardening or cracking, rub the leather parts with a damp sponge and saddle soap. A thorough coating of neatsfoot oil is excellent now and then.

Good tack is expensive and should be cared for properly. Tack should be cleaned after every use and should be stored hanging up, in a dry place.

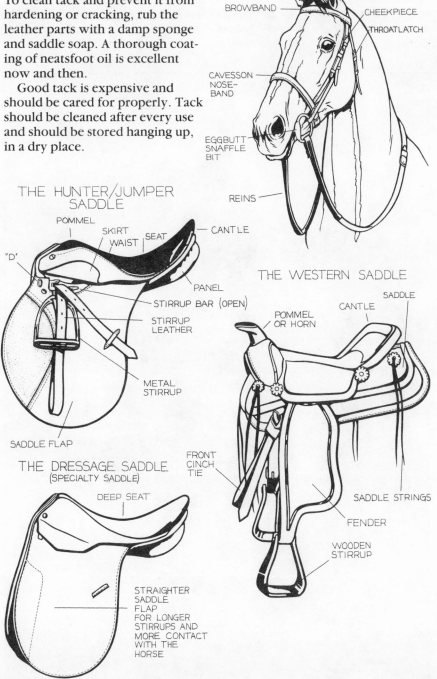

SNAFFLE BRIDLE

BROWBAND

CHEEKPIECE

THROATLATCH

CAVESSON NOSE-BAND

EGGBUTT SNAFFLE BIT

REINS

THE HUNTER/JUMPER SADDLE

POMMEL

SKIRT

WAIST

SEAT

CANTLE

"D"

PANEL

STIRRUP BAR (OPEN)

STIRRUP LEATHER

METAL STIRRUP

SADDLE FLAP

THE DRESSAGE SADDLE
(SPECIALTY SADDLE)

DEEP SEAT

STRAIGHTER SADDLE FLAP FOR LONGER STIRRUPS AND MORE CONTACT WITH THE HORSE

THE WESTERN SADDLE

SADDLE

CANTLE

POMMEL OR HORN

SADDLE STRINGS

FENDER

WOODEN STIRRUP

FRONT CINCH TIE

Rider of the Month

Diana Billes began riding in pony club when she was ten years old. Now, at the age of 19, she is one of Canada's top junior dressage riders. In 1982 she won the gold medal at the Junior North American Continental Championships.

JUNE

If you are going riding alone, always let someone know where you are going and when you expect to return.

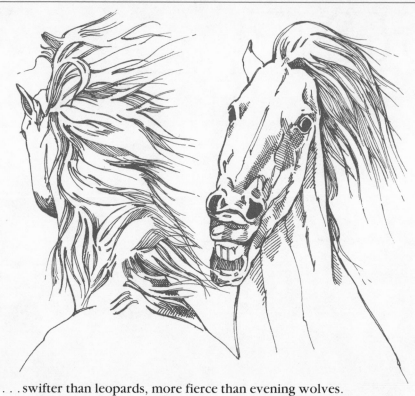

. . . swifter than leopards, more fierce than evening wolves.

Habakkuk, *Old Testament*

JUNE

The oldest European riding schools or *maneges*, where equestrian sports and equestrian masters were developed, are Versailles and Saumur in France, the Spanish Riding School of Vienna in Austria and the school at Hanover, West Germany. The European riders' dominance in equitation today can be attributed to their old and well-developed links to these schools.

EXERCISES IN THE SADDLE

These exercises can be done while you are in the saddle and will help improve your balance and coordination. Once you have mastered the exercises while the horse is standing still, try them while the horse is at a walk.

Never do these exercises on a young or inexperienced horse.

1) Keeping your upper and lower body still, turn your head as far as you can–first to the left, then to the right. Imagine that there is a string attached to the top of your head, pulling you straight up. Take slow, deep breaths. Repeat ten times to each side.

2) Hold your arms straight out at shoulder height. Swing your upper body to the left, then to the right. As you are doing this, try making small circles with your arms, first forward, then backward. Repeat ten times to each side.

3) Take your feet out of the stirrups and lift your left leg straight out away from the horse, keeping your toes pointing forward. Repeat with the right leg. Then try both legs together. Repeat the whole exercise five times.

4) With your feet out of the stirrups, rotate your feet at the ankles, first in one direction, then the other. Repeat five times.

5) Swinging your right arm in a wide arc, try to touch your left anklebone with your right hand. Make sure your foot does not come up to meet your hand, and try not to let your right leg slip backward. Repeat to the other side. Do this whole exercise five times.

6) Cross your arms at your chest and slowly lower your upper body backward to the horse's rump. Try not to let your legs slip forward. Return to an upright position. Repeat five times. This is a great exercise for your stomach muscles. If you feel any pain in your lower back or neck, stop.

7) Lean slightly forward and keep your head up and shoulders straight. Push your feet into the stirrups and raise your seat about two inches off the saddle. Then lower it gently. Repeat ten times.

Caution!

Never do these exercises without an instructor standing by.

Things to do in
JULY 19___

Date		16	
1		17	
2		18	
3		19	
4		20	
5		21	
6		22	
7		23	
8		24	
9		25	
10		26	
11		27	
12		28	
13		29	
14		30	
15		31	

The atmosphere at the showground was wonderful to me. I breathed it into my pores. Everywhere were horses and horse people. Unabashed, I listened in on conversations, hearing things like conformation, style and gait discussed, words that I didn't completely understand but was determined I would soon. I would get books from the library and read up on everything there was to know about horses. I saw girls my own age, slim as reeds in their peaked velvet hard hats, waisted jackets and jodhpurs, riding beautiful horses. They were so sure of themselves, blessed with good looks and poise. They inhabited a different world from mine, a world that I could only guess at . . .

Diana Walker, *The Year of the Horse*

JULY

The first iron horseshoes were used by the Celts in Britain nearly 2,000 years ago.

Three times [Gandalf] whistled; and then faint and far off it seemed to them that they heard the whinny of a horse borne up from the plains upon the eastern wind. They waited wondering. Before long there came the sound of hoofs.... "That is Shadowfax.... Does he not shine like silver, and run as smoothly as a swift stream? He has come for me: the horse of the White Rider. We are going to battle together."

Even as the old wizard spoke, the great horse came striding up the slope towards them; his coat was glistening and his mane flowing in the wind of his speed. ... As soon as Shadowfax saw Gandalf, he checked his pace and whinnied loudly; then trotting gently forward he stooped his proud head and nuzzled his great nostrils against the old man's neck.

J.R.R. Tolkien, *The Lord of the Rings*

JULY

If your horse resists picking up a foot when you want to clean its feet or examine its shoes, push the horse's shoulder with your shoulder. This will make the horse shift its weight to the other leg.

CARING FOR YOUR HORSE

A domesticated horse is completely dependent on its owner for food, shelter, grooming and general well-being.

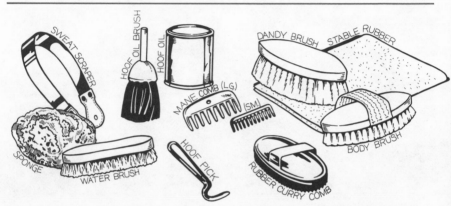

The Horse Kept at Grass

A horse that is kept in a field has the following requirements:
–Other horses for company.
–Good grazing. There should be at least one acre of good grazing for each horse. Never feed a horse grass mowings, which quickly ferment and may cause colic. During the fall and winter months when the grass is low in nutritional value, an outdoor horse may need additional hay feed. Make sure there are no poisonous plants in the field, or dangerous objects such as broken glass, tin cans or plastic bags.
–Paddocks should be harrowed with a tractor periodically to aerate the earth and distribute manure evenly over the field.

–Constant supply of fresh water. In very cold weather, ice may form on the surface of the water. This needs to be broken frequently and removed.
–Shelter. Trees or a shed are needed for shade in the summer and protection in the winter.
–Strong fencing. The fencing should be strong enough to be rubbed against, and have no pointed edges. Fences should be at least four feet high, with the bottom rail or wire at least 18 inches from the ground.

The Stabled Horse

A horse kept in a stable needs care from early morning to late at night. Looking after a stable-kept horse is a full-time job. A stabled horse needs the following:

–Daily exercise. The horse should be ridden for at least one hour, or turned out into a field for a few hours every day. Exercise should take place at least one hour after a large feed.

–Bulk food, such as hay, as well as high-protein "short" feed, such as a mixture of oats, barley, bran, or commercially packaged cubes or pellets. Horses kept indoors should also be given fresh root vegetables, such as carrots or turnips. Horses have relatively small stomachs, so they can't digest large amounts. They should be fed small amounts, three or four times a day.

–Fresh water, which should be available at all times. If water buckets are used, make sure they are emptied and rinsed out once a day.

–Bedding of straw or wood shavings, thickly laid and banked up around the walls. The stable should be cleaned out once a day; remove wet straw and droppings to prevent worms and other infections. The stall or box should be big enough for the horse to lie down comfortably.

–A blanket in cool weather.

–Fresh air without drafts.

Grooming

A horse kept in a field needs less grooming than a stable-kept horse, because heavy brushing removes the natural protective greases that an outdoor horse needs. But if a horse is kept in a stable, it should be groomed every day, after its daily exercise. It takes between 30 and 45 minutes to groom a horse properly.

–Use a hard-bristled dandy brush to remove dried dirt and sweat stains and to massage the skin. Work back from the top of the neck and always brush in the direction the coat lies with short, firm strokes. A dandy brush should never be used on the head, belly or between the thighs.

–The real cleaning work begins with a short-haired body brush, which is used to clean the skin and coat. Use firm, short, circular strokes and clean the brush with a curry comb after every few strokes.

–Comb the mane gently with a body brush or mane comb, taking care not to break any hairs.

–Clean the horse's eyes, nostrils and dock with a damp sponge.

–Brush hoof oil around and under the hooves to prevent cracking, and use a hoof pick to clean mud and stones out of the feet.

–Finally, wipe the horse all over with a clean cloth or stable rubber to make its coat shine. Use a damp cloth or water brush to smooth the tail and mane.

–(After a bath or heavy workout, a sweat scraper is sometimes used to remove excess water from the horse's coat.)

Shoeing

Horses that run wild do not need shoes because their hooves wear down naturally. But domesticated horses may be kept on too soft a surface for the hooves to wear away–if the hooves are allowed to grow too long they may become cracked or grow out of shape. Or a horse that is constantly ridden on hard roads may wear down its hooves faster than they grow. So most horses wear metal shoes to protect their feet. A horse usually needs to be re-shod every six weeks.

Rider of the Month

Hugh Graham was a champion calf roper throughout his high-school days. He has been a Grand Prix show jumper for the past ten years and in 1982 was named the Rothmans Rider of the Year, having won more Grand Prix events than any other Canadian rider.

JULY

A horse should receive injections for flu and tetanus, plus a complete checkup, twice a year. Horses should be wormed every three months.

Round-hoof'd, short-jointed, fetlocks shag and long,
Broad breast, full eye, small head and nostril wide,
High crest, short ears, straight legs and passing strong,
Thin mane, thick tail, broad buttock, tender hide:
  Look, what a horse should have he did not lack,
  Save a proud rider on so proud a back.

William Shakespeare, ''Venus and Adonis''

JULY

Riding is becoming a popular sport for the disabled, providing therapy and pleasure. Riding enables many physically handicapped people to become mobile.

Things to do in
AUGUST 19__

Date		16	
1		17	
2		18	
3		19	
4		20	
5		21	
6		22	
7		23	
8		24	
9		25	
10		26	
11		27	
12		28	
13		29	
14		30	
15		31	

Miss Ada bent her head suddenly and rubbed the itch off her right nostril on to her leg, and as she did it she flashed a robust, contemptuous look at Velvet. "Is there sugar?" said the look, "or no sugar? I want no subtleties, no sentimentalities. I don't care about your state of heart, your wretched conscience-prickings, your ambitious desires. Is there sugar or no sugar? State your reasons for coming to see me and leave me to brood."

Velvet produced a piece of sugar and the pony bent her head round with a look of insolence, as though she still suspected the sugar to be an imitation lump. She took it with her lips, but she pressed her old teeth for a minute on the child's palm, and at this trick, as old as Velvet's childhood, Velvet thrust her arms over the sagging backbone and buried her face among the knobbles of the spine. The pony munched her lump stolidly, flirting her head up and down as though she were fishing for extra grains high up among her teeth.

Enid Bagnold, *National Velvet* (illustrated by Laurian Jones)

AUGUST

Some horses that are stabled for long periods may develop the nervous habit of "weaving" or swaying from side to side. This habit wastes a lot of energy and is also likely to be picked up by other horses. Keep a "weaver" out of sight of other horses.

The head was that of the wildest of all wild creatures–a stallion born wild–and it was beautiful, savage, splendid. A stallion with a wonderful physical perfection . . .

Walter Farley, *The Black Stallion*

AUGUST

Some horses "crib" or nibble on the edges of their stalls. This is a natural tendency, like thumb-sucking in children, but it can cause a horse to swallow air and may cause stomach disorders. Like weaving, cribbing is often the result of boredom and lack of exercise. Take your horse out regularly and try to give it company. If it can't be near other horses, cats can make good companions.

RIDING YOUR HORSE

Preparing to Ride

Always try to approach a horse gradually from the front and speak to it calmly as you approach.

To lead a horse, walk on the left (near) side of it, holding a shank about 18 inches from the head, in your right hand. Hold the long end of the shank in your left hand, but don't wind it around your hands in case the horse suddenly bolts. Never start a tug of war with a horse–it will develop the bad habit of constantly pulling back. Extend your right arm while leading, keeping the horse's head away so the horse will not step on your heels.

To mount a horse, move close to its left shoulder, facing its tail. Take the reins with your left hand and grasp the mane. With your right hand, grasp the stirrup and place your left foot in it. Be careful not to jab the horse with your toe. Then grasp the front or far side of the saddle and swing up, pushing off your right foot and pulling your body up with your arms. Try to ease yourself into the saddle; never land with a thump, because this is very hard on the horse's back.

Sit in the deepest part of the saddle with your back relaxed but straight and your eyes facing straight ahead. Always try to avoid looking down. The ball of your foot should rest on the stirrup bar and your toes should point straight ahead. Knees and thighs should be kept against the saddle, ready to keep you steady.

To hold the reins correctly, think of carrying them, rather than gripping them. Your fists should be rounded with thumbs on top, wrists relaxed and in line with the elbows. Hands should be held just above the withers.

To dismount, take the reins in your left hand and remove your right foot from the stirrup. Put your left hand on the horse's withers and your right hand on the front of the saddle. Stand up in your left stirrup, and swing your right leg over the horse's quarters. Slide your left foot out of the stirrup and slide to the ground, pushing yourself slightly away from the horse as you do.

The Aids

A rider communicates with a horse by means of four aids: the weight, legs, reins and voice.

Your weight affects the horse through its back as you shift your weight in various maneuvers. It is important to learn to sit in a quiet, balanced position and not use your weight unknowingly or indiscriminately. Every rider should develop an "independent" seat, i.e., be able to remain in the saddle without supporting him/herself with the reins.

Squeezing with both legs behind the girth encourages a horse to move forward. Your legs should never lose contact with the horse's side.

The hands on the reins exert influence on the horse's mouth, thereby controlling the horse's frame and the tempo of the gait.

The voice is used to calm or encourage a horse or give it confidence. Horses are highly sensitive to sound, and they can learn to recognize different tones of voice.

Training Your Horse

Training a horse requires great patience–you must never push the horse and must proceed from one step to another very gradually. Several short training periods are better than one long one. Never punish a horse for disobedience unless you are sure that it has really understood what you wanted it to do. Punishment and praise must be given immediately in order for the horse to associate it with the action.

Rider of the Month

Kathy Kusner has been a member of the U.S. Equestrian Team since 1961 and has competed in three Olympic Games. She has been voted Horse-woman of the Year and was also the first licensed female jockey in the world. Kathy is shown here on the legendary show jumper, "Untouch-able."

AUGUST

Always run your stirrups up the stirrup straps or leathers as soon as you dismount. A horse can get its teeth caught in them if it is biting at a fly. And if the horse should get away from you, the swinging stirrups will only encourage it to run faster and faster.

My horses understand me tolerably well; I converse with them at least four hours every day. They are strangers to bridle or saddle; they live in great amity with me, and friendship to each other.

Jonathan Swift, *Gulliver's Travels* (illustrated by Aldren Watson)

AUGUST

To be well dressed, a horse in North America traditionally wears its mane on the right side of its neck. Wet and brush the mane hairs to get them to lie flat.

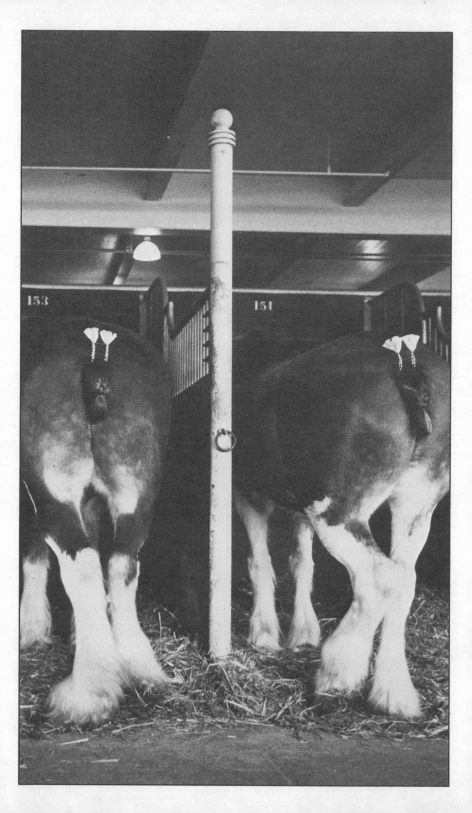

Things to do in
SEPTEMBER 19__

Date	16
1	17
2	18
3	19
4	20
5	21
6	22
7	23
8	24
9	25
10	26
11	27
12	28
13	29
14	30
15	

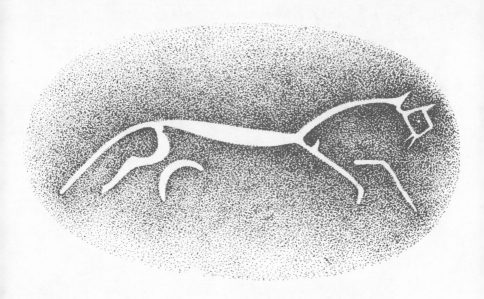

Then out from the rest, one took the lead, mane streaming, tail streaming, white against the gathering storm, whiter than the secret chalk below the grass, whiter than thorn blossom. For a few heartbeats of time she was his to see, with the skein of· darker mares following after. And then, from out of the heart of the piled clouds, came a licking tongue of lightning. For an instant the mare seemed made of white fire, and the fire of her burned into the inmost self of the Chieftain's youngest son as a brand burns into the hide of a yearling colt, leaving a mark which is never quite lost.

Then she flung round, snorting with fear, and was gone over the lip of the Downs, the rest after her. And in the same instant, there was a crack of thunder like a whiplash, that turned into the roar of the skies falling, and boomed and echoed away among the combes and hollows of the Chalk. And Lubrin's father flung a dark wing of his cloak over him as the rain came hissing towards them along the dry ground.

Later, the sun came out again and everything was shining. But that was not what Lubrin remembered. He remembered the white mare, the dream.

Rosemary Sutcliff, *Sun Horse, Moon Horse* (illustrated by Shirley Felts)

SEPTEMBER

At horse shows, winners' ribbons come in traditional colors. The four-striped ribbons are for Grand Champions and the three-striped ribbons are for Champions. In the United States, blue, red and yellow ribbons are awarded for first, second and third prize respectively. In Canada the red ribbon is awarded for first prize, the blue ribbon for second prize and the white ribbon for third prize.

With flowing tail and flying mane,
Wide nostrils–never stretched with pain–
Mouths bloodless to the bit or rein,
And feet that iron never shod,
And flanks unscarred by spur or rod,
A thousand horse, the wild, the free,
Like waves that follow o'er the sea.

Lord Byron, "Mazeppa"

SEPTEMBER

Mohammed, whose followers rode Arab horses, decreed that it was the religious duty of all Moslems to love their horses. The Koran is full of advice on horse care.

PREPARING FOR A HORSE SHOW

1) Make sure you are completely familiar with the rules of the competition you are entering. Obtain a rule book and study it carefully in advance. Before you enter a competition, try to attend the event first as a spectator so you will be familiar with the procedure, dress and level of competition. Be sensible in your choice of shows and classes. Even average riders and horses can have fun and benefit by entering local shows and gymkhana events.

2) Eligibility for certain classes is based on a horse's age, height, sex, weight and past show experience. Make sure your horse is eligible for the class you are entering.

3) Make sure you dress as outlined in the rules.

4) Groom your horse carefully before a show, and have it shod about a week ahead of time. Your horse's mane, tail and shoeing should comply with the show's regulations.

5) Allow twice as much time as you think you will need to get ready and drive to the show. Rushing will make the horse and yourself tense. Try to arrive at the show early, to allow your horse time to become accustomed to the surroundings.

6) Make a checklist of all necessary equipment ahead of time, to make sure nothing is forgotten. It will be a big asset if you can arrive at the competition calm, neat and organized.

7) Label all your equipment and tack.

8) Make your horse's travel arrangements well in advance. You will need to rent or borrow a horse trailer. Your horse may also need additional protection when it is traveling, such as a blanket and traveling bandages.

9) Make sure your horse is warmed up before the event.

10) Don't overdo it. Don't try to enter every event in the show. Four classes a day is more than enough.

11) You never know when a judge will glance in your direction, so consider yourself on show from the minute you enter the ring. Try to stay calm and poised. Don't chat with your friends or think about the spectators. Concentrate only on your ride.

12) Respect the unwritten rules of show-ring etiquette. Never put down another rider or another horse, never complain about the courses or imperfect conditions and never dispute the decision of the judges.

Braiding

In horse shows, horses are often shown with braided manes and tails. Small braids can give the impression that a horse's neck is longer than it really is; a few thick braids tend to shorten the horse's neck.

To braid a mane, dampen it with your fingers and comb it. Separate each three-inch-thick section into three and then make neat braids. Turn the ends of the braids under, then fasten with elastic or heavy thread. Some people also braid the horse's forelock, sometimes winding colored ribbons into the braids. To braid a horse's tail, take hairs from the middle and each side of the tail. Do not try to incorporate all the tail hairs into the braid. Braiding a horse's tail neatly requires lots of practice and considerable patience.

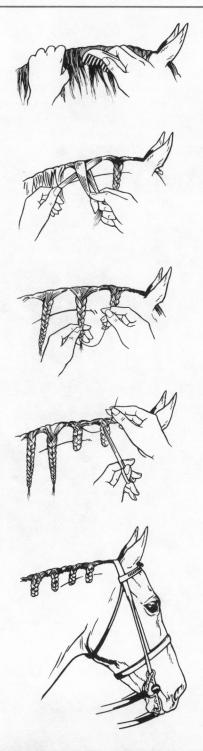

Rider of the Month

Bernie Traurig started his riding career by taking 25-cent pony rides at a local farm. At the age of 18 he began working with the U.S. Equestrian Team. Over the years he has won the National Horse Show Grand Prix three times, as well as the U.S. Open Jumping Championships. He is shown riding "Eadenvale" at Bromont, Quebec.

SEPTEMBER

Thoroughbred horses are renowned for their courage and nerve. During a New Orleans race, Kentucky Derby winner Black Gold snapped a bone in one of his forelegs while racing in on the homestretch. Despite his jockey's efforts to pull the horse up, Black Gold lunged ahead to finish the race on three legs.

A horse gallops with his lung,
Perseveres with his heart,
And wins with his character.

Tesio

SEPTEMBER

Do not wear loose-fitting clothing while riding. It may become caught in bushes or may flap around and distract your horse.

MY DREAM HORSE

Watch for your dream horse at horse
shows and in magazines and books. Keep a
photograph of your dream horse here.

Name

Breed

Size

Sex   Age

Description, color and markings

Disposition and character

Equipment I'll need

Daily routine

Stable plan

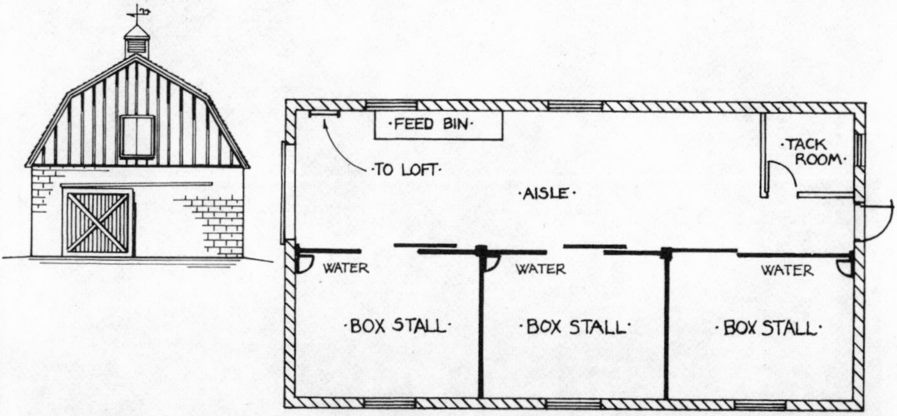

FEED BIN

TO LOFT

TACK ROOM

AISLE

WATER

WATER

WATER

BOX STALL

BOX STALL

BOX STALL

Things to do in
OCTOBER 19—

Date		16	
1		17	
2		18	
3		19	
4		20	
5		21	
6		22	
7		23	
8		24	
9		25	
10		26	
11		27	
12		28	
13		29	
14		30	
15		31	

As Paul and Maureen stood inside the big corral, looking at Misty, they knew she was the finest-blooded foal in the world. Oh, the beauty of her! She was neither silver nor gold. She was both. And she had a funny white blaze that started down the left side of her face, then did a right-about and covered her whole muzzle. It gave her a look of wonderment and surprise.

They could have gazed at her forever, exclaiming over her gold eyelashes, her pink underlip, her funny knobby knees, her short flappy tail, the furry insides of her ears. But suddenly Paul was aware of an uneasy feeling, as though someone were eyeing him. Then he felt a hot breath on the back of his neck. Slowly he turned his head and came face to face with the Pied Piper.

For an instant neither the stallion nor the boy winked an eyelash. Pied Piper stared fixedly at Paul from under his long forelock. He was like a man peering out from ambush. Paul could see the white ring around the stallion's eyes, the red lining of his nostrils, the ears flattened. He could smell the wildness. He sensed that one false move, and a darting foreleg might knock him down as if he were a cornstalk. . . .

Marguerite Henry, *Misty of Chincoteague* (illustrated by Wesley Dennis)

OCTOBER

The most famous of Napoleon's chargers, Marengo, was captured by the British at Waterloo. He was 22 years old at the time and eventually lived to be 38. His skeleton is preserved in the museum of the Royal United Services Institution in London.

They were just begin-
ning to descend; and it
was evident that the
horse, whether of her
own will or of his (the
latter being the more
likely), knew so well
the reckless perform-
ance expected of her
that she hardly
required a hint from
behind.

Thomas Hardy,
Tess of the D'Urbervilles

OCTOBER

Even for quiet pleasure riding, two items of clothing are essential: a properly fitting hard hat (such as the velveteen-covered hunt cap), ideally with a chin strap, to protect your head in case of a fall, and a fitted, heeled shoe to protect your foot and prevent it from sliding through the stirrups. Sneakers, loafers or shoes with heavy, ridged soles are unsafe for riding.

SKETCHING HORSES

by Elaine Macpherson

The horse combines beauty, symmetry and power. It is easy to see but not so easy to capture on paper. Study the photo below and the line illustration beside it. Then practice sketching the form with pencil or charcoal. Don't worry about the exact duplication–a loose, expressive line can say it all.

Some tips:
– Take every opportunity to study a living model—in motion, at rest, in winter and summer, in good light and bad light. Look at the horse's surface and the forms beneath. Touch the horse and memorize its textures: the softness of a muzzle, the hardness of a hoof.
– Practice often–from memory and life.
– Experiment with different media such as pencil, watercolor, charcoal and oil paint.
– Study the way Toulouse-Lautrec drew horses. Look at the works of artists George Stubbs and Sir Alfred J. Munnings.
– Wake up to a favorite horse picture in the morning–a photo or a painting. Try to see something new in it each day. Change the picture every month.

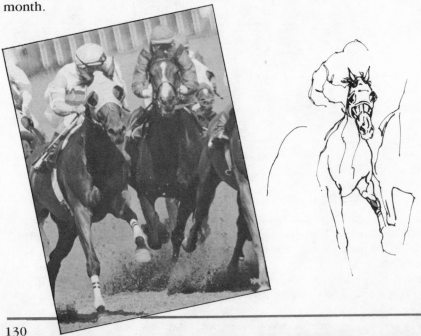

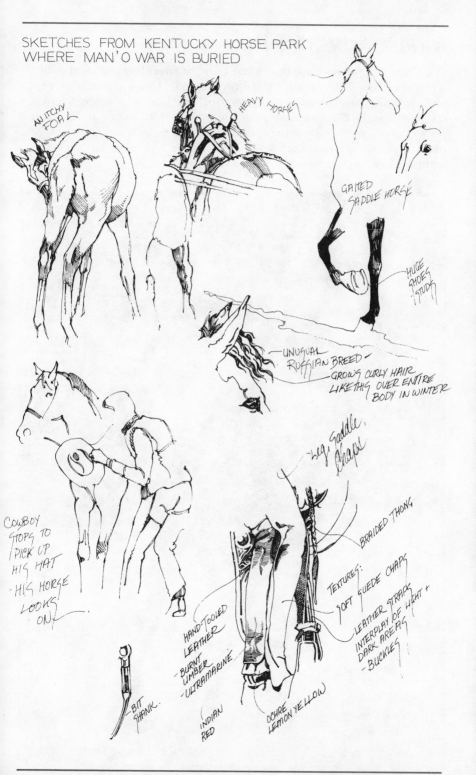

AN ITCHY
FOAL

HEAVY HORSES

GAITED
SADDLE HORSE

HUGE
SHOES
+ STUDS

— UNUSUAL
RUSSIAN BREED —
GROWS CURLY HAIR
LIKE THIS OVER ENTIRE
BODY IN WINTER

Leg. Saddle.
Chaps.

BRAIDED THONG

TEXTURES:
SOFT SUEDE CHAPS

LEATHER STRAPS
INTERPLAY OF LIGHT +
DARK AREAS
— BUCKLES

COWBOY
STOPS TO
PICK UP
HIS HAT
- HIS HORSE
LOOKS
ON.

HAND-TOOLED
LEATHER

— BURNT
UMBER
-ULTRAMARINE

BIT
SHANK.

INDIAN
RED

OCHRE
LEMON YELLOW

Rider of the Month

Eva-Maria Pracht was born in Germany and began riding at a local stable when she was 15. A year later she won a regional junior championship, and eventually she became an international-level dressage rider, winning six medals at the German championships. "It is so important to love and respect the horse that you ride and train, and to make it your best friend," she says. "Only then will success arrive on your doorstep." She is shown here on her horse "Van Eick."

OCTOBER

The world's tiniest horse is the Falabella, a pony breed from Argentina. These good-natured ponies are often kept as pets, have long, silky coats and are less than seven hands high.

Boot, saddle, to horse, and away!
Robert Browning, ''Boot and Saddle''

OCTOBER

The best-known mounted police force in the world is the Royal Canadian Mounted Police, which was formed in 1873. Today the Mounties are mechanized, but for ceremonial parades and their famous Musical Ride (a special group dressage performance) they still train horsemen and breed their own horses – quality black horses between 15.3 and 16.2 hands high.

Things to do in
NOVEMBER *19__*

Date	16
1	17
2	18
3	19
4	20
5	21
6	22
7	23
8	24
9	25
10	26
11	27
12	28
13	29
14	30
15	

The next twelve minutes were indescribable. I lost consciousness of everything around me. I was alone with my horse, going through the most difficult dressage test in the world. The stillness, the communication between the two of us, as I asked for the different movements, and as he gave; an extra pressure, a silent rebuke, an unseen praising, a firm correction; all these passed between us as though through telegraph wires. In the piaffe I sensed the difficulty Bonheur was having to pull his feet out of the very soft footing. As he was not experienced enough for me to risk upsetting him about it, I let him move on. The pirouettes also became suddenly hazardous, and I felt him slip on one of them. We neared the end; the flying changes were coming. I headed him across the diagonal, one two, two two, three two, four two, five two, six two, seven two, eight two, nine two! We had completed without mistake the nine flying changes on every second stride. Again we had swung around to begin the second diagonal. One, two, three, four, five, six, seven, eight, nine, ten, eleven, twelve, thirteen, fourteen, fifteen! I breathed a sigh of relief when the difficult one-tempo changes were behind me. Bonheur had come through strongly once more and it was with much happiness and relief that we walked out of the ring. Half-laughing, half-crying, I could only whisper to the great horse that had seen me through to the end, "It's all over now, it's all over. . . ."

Christilot Hanson Boylen, *Canadian Entry*

NOVEMBER

Although the term *dressage* did not come into use until the early eighteenth century, the sport goes back to the Greek historian and philosopher Xenophon, who in the third century B.C. described how to obtain the cooperation of the horse and teach it to use its natural paces to advantage.

To learn all that a horse could teach, was a world of knowledge, but only a beginning. . . . Look into a horse's eye and you instantly know if you can trust him.

Mary O'Hara, *The Catch Colt*

NOVEMBER

Competitive riding is one of the few sports that allows men and women to compete against each other. Competitive riders sometimes train as much as eight hours a day, 52 weeks a year.

OLYMPIC EQUESTRIAN EVENTS

Three equestrian sports are recognized by the International Olympic Committee: the Grand Prix de Dressage Event, the Grand Prix Jumping Event, and the Three-Day Event.

Grand Prix de Dressage

Dressage is the art of guiding a horse through maneuvers in a graceful and harmonious manner, without emphasis on the use of reins, hands or legs. Dressage competition can be compared to dancing on horseback. The horse and rider must complete a certain series of precise movements, within a time limit, and at certain markers placed around the competition ring.

The dressage competition ring is a rectangle, 66 feet by 198 feet. There are five judges positioned around the ring and each judge independently scores each ride, giving a mark between 0 and 10 for each movement. Marks from 0 to 4 are poor, 5 or 6 is average, 7 to 9 denotes varying degrees of excellence and the "10" is given when the judge feels that the horse and rider have come close to perfection in a certain maneuver. The rider and horse receiving the highest total score win the competition.

The judges are looking for smoothness, accuracy and brilliance of movement. It should never appear that the rider is making the horse do something by force; the horse should perform willingly with the lightest of controls.

The Grand Prix test used at the Olympics has a time limit of 10 minutes and is made up of 39 maneuvers.

Grand Prix Jumping

The Grand Prix jumping competition tests the horse and rider over a "course" of jumps that must be completed within a specified time.

Penalties are given for knocking down an obstacle (4 faults) or for stopping or running out at an obstacle (3 faults). There are time faults if the horse and rider go over the time allowed.

The courses are extremely difficult, testing the horse's ability to jump straight up-and-down obstacles (verticals) and wide jumps (oxers). One of the most difficult aspects of any Grand Prix is the "combination," where the horse must jump through a series of two or three fences usually made up of verticals and spreads (jumps that are wide as well as high), with only one or two strides between them.

The horse and rider with the lowest number of penalties win the competition.

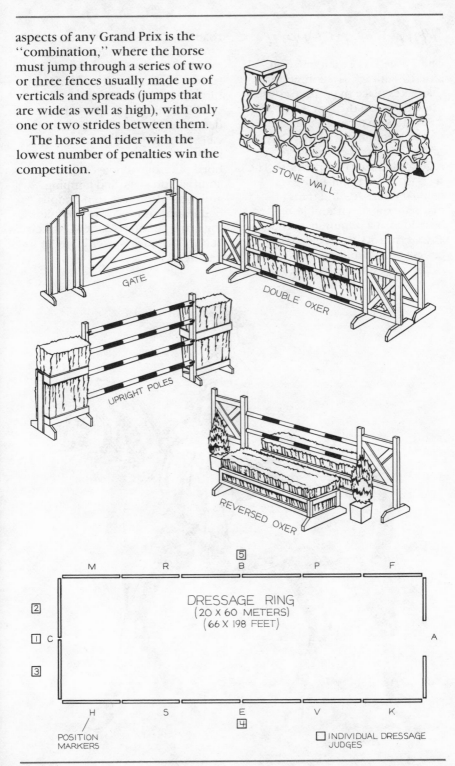

STONE WALL

GATE

DOUBLE OXER

UPRIGHT POLES

REVERSED OXER

DRESSAGE RING
(20 X 60 METERS)
(66 X 198 FEET)

M   R   5 B   P   F

2

1 C   A

3

H   S   E   V   K
           4

POSITION
MARKERS

☐ INDIVIDUAL DRESSAGE
JUDGES

Three-Day Event

The Three-Day Event or "Combined Training" is a competition that takes place over three consecutive days. On the first day, horses and riders go through a dressage test of medium difficulty. They are scored in a manner similar to any regular dressage competition. The second day is a four-phase test made up of roads and trails (a marked course without jumps, to be ridden at a minimum speed–usually a fast trot), a steeplechase course of $2^1/_2$ miles (covered at a gallop over 8 to 12 fences), more roads and trails and then a cross-country obstacle course. The third day is a show-jumping test over a relatively short course of medium difficulty (10 to 12 fences).

The Three-Day Event is a very demanding equestrian sport and calls for a very high level of riding ability. To be a successful event horse, the animal must show basic ability in dressage and jumping, and must also show tremendous endurance and speed to complete the cross-country segment, which at the Olympics is over 20 miles in length.

DRESSAGE
PHASE

STEEPLECHASE/
CROSS-COUNTRY
PHASE

STADIUM
JUMPING
PHASE

Rider of the Month

Jim Elder is one of North America's leading equestrians and one of Canada's top athletes of all time. He has taken part in international competitions for thirty years and has brought home gold, silver and bronze medals from the Pan-American Games, World Championships and Olympic Games. He is shown riding "Volunteer," a Thoroughbred chestnut gelding.

NOVEMBER

Experts say that it takes even a very talented horse four years of training to be brought up to the Grand Prix level by a master trainer. However, it can take a rider at least ten years to learn to go through a Grand Prix de Dressage test.

A little neglect may breed mischief; . . . for want of a nail, the shoe was lost; for want of a shoe the horse was lost; for want of a horse the rider was lost.

Benjamin Franklin, *Poor Richard's Almanack*

NOVEMBER

A rider's age is often a factor in the way he or she is judged in competition. In international competition especially, a young competitor must expect to be judged extremely hard. The most highly rated competitors in the Grand Prix de Dressage competition, for instance, are often in their forties or fifties.

Things to do in
DECEMBER 19—

Date	16
1	17
2	18
3	19
4	20
5	21
6	22
7	23
8	24
9	25
10	26
11	27
12	28
13	29
14	30
15	31

I cannot say how long I had slept, nor what time in the night it was, but I woke up feeling very uncomfortable, though I hardly knew why. I got up: the air seemed all thick and choking. I heard Ginger coughing, and one of the other horses moved about restlessly. It was quite dark, and I could see nothing; but the stable was full of smoke, and I hardly knew how to breathe.

The trap door had been left open, and I thought that was the place from which the smoke came. I listened and heard a soft, rushing sort of noise, and a low crackling and snapping. I did not know what it was, but there was something in the sound so strange that it made me tremble all over. The other horses were now all awake; some were pulling at their halters, others were stamping. . . . The fresh air that had come in through the open door made it easier to breathe, but the rushing sound overhead grew louder, and as I looked upward, through the bars of my empty rack, I saw a red light flickering on the wall. Then I heard a cry of "Fire!" outside, and the old ostler came quietly and quickly in. He got one horse out, and went to another; but the flames were playing round the trap door, and the roaring overhead was dreadful.

Anna Sewell, *Black Beauty* (illustrated by Lucy Kemp-Welch)

DECEMBER

"Walk the first mile out and the last mile in." Give your horse time to warm up after leaving the stable and time to cool down before returning. Your horse should always return to the stable cool and dry.

It was not the silver cup standing above the windblown tablecloth that Velvet saw–but the perfection of accomplishment, the silken co-operation between two actors, the horse and the human . . .

Enid Bagnold, *National Velvet* (illustrated by Laurian Jones)

DECEMBER

For the official hunt season, special livery is worn. Men who meet hunt club requirements are allowed to wear scarlet jackets. Official hunting gear for women is the black cutaway jacket. The white stock is worn to serve as a sling or bandage in case of an accident.

BIRTH OF A FOAL

Mares come into heat (estrus) every three weeks from early spring to midsummer (the official Thoroughbred breeding season runs from February 15 to July 15). Heat lasts between five and seven days.

A foal grows inside its mother for about eleven months (335 to 350 days) and there is usually only one foal. Foals are born in late spring or early summer.

The fetus develops within an outer membrane that protects it against blows or shock. The fetus is nourished by a flow of blood between the mare and the foal, and grows most rapidly during the second half of the pregnancy.

Before a mare gives birth, grooves may appear on either side of the root of the tail, caused by the relaxation of muscles to ease the passage of the foal. Her udder will increase in size and she may begin to sweat and become restless, swishing her tail and looking at her flanks. You may be able to see the movements of the foal against her abdominal wall.

Most mares give birth in the early hours of the morning. You can see the contractions begin. They may be 5 to 10 minutes apart to start, but will gradually become more frequent (every 30 seconds). Labor usually lasts no more than three hours.

The first thing you will see is the grayish outer membrane of the protective sac. The membrane will break and in a normal birth, you will then see the foal's forelegs, followed by the head, chest and shoulders. The hind legs emerge last, and then the umbilical cord breaks naturally or is cut. The actual birth only takes about 12 minutes. Within an hour, the placenta–the layers of membrane that have nourished and protected the foal inside the mare–will be expelled.

At birth, a foal's eyes are open, and it is covered with a full coat. Immediately after the birth, the mare should begin to lick the foal. Within an hour or two after the birth, the foal should stand up and begin sucking milk.

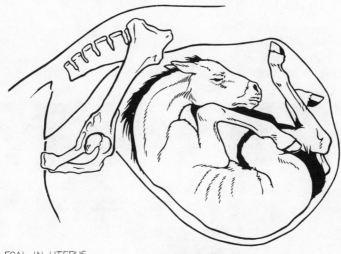

FOAL IN UTERUS

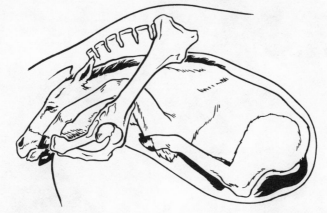

FOAL EMERGING

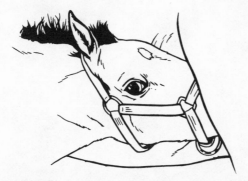

FOAL NURSING

Rider of the Month

Lorraine Stubbs started riding at the age of 13, at the local pony club. She has ridden on two Olympic teams and now breeds and trains dressage and Thoroughbred horses at her farm in Rockwood, Ontario. She is shown riding her Trakehner stallion "Condus."

DECEMBER

A whip or crop is normally used to make the horse more responsive to the rider's leg. It should be used on the horse's barrel, directly behind the rider's calf.

There is no secret so close as that between a rider and his horse.

R.S. Surtees, *Mr. Sponge's Sporting Tour*

DECEMBER

Although most horses are flown to international competitions, flying can be dangerous for horses. If a confused and frightened animal becomes violent, years of training can go for nothing. A revolver is always kept on board and will be used without hesitation if a panicked horse endangers the plane's safety.

BREEDS CHECKLIST

Many of the horses you see are crossbred, but it can be fun to try to spot different breeds. Identifying breeds will also sharpen your eye to distinguish the special physical features of different horses.

Use this list to keep a record of the purebred horses you see at horse shows, racetracks or stud farms.

Breed	Date	Place
Akhal-Teke		
American Saddlebred		
Andalusian		
Anglo-Arab		
Anglo-Norman		
Appaloosa		
Arab		
Camargue Pony		
Chincoteague		
Cleveland Bay		
Clydesdale		
Connemara		
Danish Sportshorse		
Dartmoor Pony		
Dutch Draft		
Dutch Warmblood		
Exmoor Pony		
Falabella		
Fell Pony		
Fjord Pony		
Friesian		
Gelderland		
Hackney		

Breed	Date	Place
Haflinger Pony		
Hanoverian		
Hanoverian Warmblood		
Holstein Warmblood		
Iceland Pony		
Lipizzaner		
Lusitano		
Morgan		
Mustang		
New Forest Pony		
Oldenburg Warmblood		
Palomino		
Paso Fino		
Percheron		
Pinto		
Pony of the Americas		
Quarter Horse		
Shetland Pony		
Shire		
Standardbred		
Swedish Warmblood		
Swiss Warmblood		
Tennessee Walking Horse		
Thoroughbred		
Trakehner Warmblood		
Waler Australian Horse		
Welsh Cob		
Welsh Mountain Pony		
Westphalian Warmblood		
Wielkopolski (Polish Warmblood)		

Glossary

Break To train a horse to accept a rider in the saddle.

Broodmare A female horse or mare chosen to produce foals year after year.

Canter A controlled, three-beat gallop.

Cavaletti Small wooden cross poles that can usually be set at three different heights under 12 inches. Used in the schooling of both horse and rider.

Cob A short, compact horse or pony not more than 15 hands (60 inches) high.

Collect To bring a horse's body into balance, with greater weight on the hindquarters.

Colt A male horse under four years of age.

Dam A female horse or mare that has had foals.

Dressage The breaking and basic gymnastic schooling of a horse. Also refers to precision movements performed by disciplined, well-trained horses in dressage competition.

Equitation The art of horseback riding.

Estrus The period when a mare is sexually active and will accept mating with a stallion.

Feather The hair on the back of the fetlocks.

Filly A female horse under four years of age.

Foal A male or female horse up to one year old.

Gait The foot movements of a horse used at different paces—walk, trot, canter and gallop.

Gallop A fast, bounding natural gait.

Gelding A castrated male horse.

Gymkhana A horse or pony event where mounted games and races are carried out by children.

Hack A well-behaved and well-schooled riding horse of light build. Also refers to recreational riding.

Hunter A strong, fit horse capable of galloping cross-country and jumping well.

Jog A slow, even trot.

Light horse Any horse suitable for riding that is not a Thoroughbred or a draft breed.

Longeing Working a horse from the ground on a circle at the end of a long canvas rein.

Mare A female horse or pony that is more than four years of age.

Near side The left side of a horse (when one is sitting on the horse). Usually a horse is mounted and tacked up from the near side.

Off side The right side of a horse, when one is sitting on the horse.

Posting While trotting, the act of raising and lowering oneself into the saddle in rhythm with the horse's movements.

Purebred A horse of unmixed breed. Not a Thoroughbred, which is the name of a specific breed.

Seat The position of the rider in the saddle. Refers to the posture and attitude of the entire body.

Shank A leather strap (approximately six to eight feet long) used to lead a horse.

Shy When a horse swerves away from an unexpected object.

Sire The male parent of a horse.

Stallion An uncastrated male horse over four years old.

Steeplechase A race run over fences on a course that is about five miles long.

Stud A breeding stallion.

Tack Riding equipment, including the saddle, bridle, pad, girth, stirrups, etc.

Trot The diagonal movement of the legs at a moderate gait.

Walk A slow gait in which the horse's feet maintain a four-beat rhythm.

Western riding A type of riding using a Western saddle and bridle or hackamore. Used by cowboys for range work and cattle cutting.

Reading List

Fiction

Bagnold, Enid. *National Velvet*. New York: William Morrow, 1949.

Doty, Jean S. *Summer Pony*. New York: Macmillan, 1973.

Farley, Walter. *The Black Stallion*. New York: Random House, 1941.

_____. *The Black Stallion Returns*. New York: Random House, 1945.

_____. *Man o' War*. New York: Random House, 1962.

Goble, Paul. *The Girl Who Loved Wild Horses*. Scarsdale, New York: Bradbury, 1978.

Henry, Marguerite. *King of the Wind*. Chicago: Rand McNally, 1948.

_____. *Misty of Chincoteague*. Chicago: Rand McNally, 1947.

McHargue, Georgess. *The Horseman's Word*. New York: Delacorte, 1981.

Mitchell, Elynne. *Silver Brumbies of the South*. London: Granada, 1979.

Morey, Walt. *Runaway Stallion*. New York: Dutton, 1973.

_____. *Year of the Black Pony*. New York: Dutton, 1976.

O'Hara, Mary. *The Catch Colt*. Toronto: McClelland and Stewart, 1981.

_____. *The Green Grass of Wyoming*. New York: Harper and Row, 1946.

Peyton, K.M. *Flambards in Summer*. Toronto: Penguin, 1969.

_____. *Fly-by-Night*. London: Sparrow, 1981.

Sewell, Anna. *Black Beauty*. New York: Dutton, 1963.

Sutcliff, Rosemary. *Sun Horse, Moon Horse*. London: Hodder and Stoughton, 1977.

Treadgold, Mary. *No Ponies*. London: Jonathan Cape, 1981.

_____. *We Couldn't Leave Dinah*. London: Jonathan Cape, 1980.

Walker, Diana. *The Year of the Horse*. New York: Abelard-Schuman, 1975.

Non-Fiction

Boylen, Christilot Hanson. *Basic Dressage for North America*. Toronto: Cumberland, 1976.

_____. *Canadian Entry*. Toronto: Clarke Irwin, 1966.

Edwards, Elwyn Hatley, and Candida Geddes. *The Complete Book of the Horse*, revised edition. Edmonton: Hurtig, 1982.

Gordon-Watson, Mary. *The Handbook of Riding*. New York: Knopf, 1982.

Hundt, Sheila Wall. *Invitation to Riding*. New York: Simon and Schuster, 1976.

Kidd, Jane. *An Illustrated Guide to Horse and Pony Care*. New York: Arco, 1981.

Morris, George H. *Hunter Seat Equitation*. Garden City, New York: Doubleday, 1971.

Podhajsky, Alois. *The Complete Training of Horse and Rider in the Principles of Classical Horsemanship*. Garden City, New York: Doubleday, 1967.

Steinkraus, William. *Riding and Jumping*, revised edition. Garden City, New York: Doubleday, 1969.

Stoneridge, M.A. *A Horse of Your Own*, revised edition. Garden City, New York: Doubleday, 1968.

Watjen, Richard L. *Dressage Riding*. Canaan, New York: J.A. Allen, 1978.

Magazines

United States

American Horseman. 257 Park Avenue South, New York, New York 10003.

American Turf Monthly. 505 Eighth Avenue, New York, New York 10018.

Arabian Horse World. 2650 East Bayshore, Palo Alto, California 94303.

Centaur. 656 Quince Orchard Road, Gaithersburg, Maryland, 20878.

The Chronicle of the Horse. P.O. Box 46, Middleburg, Virginia 22117.

Horse Action. P.O. Box 555, 41919 Moreno, Temecula, California 92390.

Horse Care. P.O. Box 555, 41919 Moreno, Temecula, California 92390.

Horse and Horseman. P.O. Box HH 34249, Camino Capistrano, Capistrano Beach, California 92624.

Horse Women. P.O. Box 555, 41919 Moreno, Temecula, California 92390.

Horseman Magazine. 5314 Bingle Road, Houston, Texas 77092.

The Quarterhorse Journal. 3014 West 10th, Amarillo, Texas 79168.

Western Horseman. 3850 North Nevada Avenue, Colorado Springs, Colorado 80933.

Canada

B.C. Horseman. 3446 Capilano Road, North Vancouver, British Columbia V7R 4H8.

The B.C. Thoroughbred. 4023 East Hastings Street, North Burnaby, British Columbia V5C 2J1.

Canada Rides. Box 6818, Station D, Calgary, Alberta T2P 2E7.

The Canadian Horse. 7240 Woodbine Avenue, Markham, Ontario L3R 1A4.

The Corinthian. 10077-C Yonge Street, Richmond Hill, Ontario L4C 1T7.

Great Britain

Horse and Pony. Bushfield House, Orton Centre, Peterborough, England.

My Horse Weekly. Box 75, East Wing, Barnards Inn, Holborn, London, England.

Pony World. Ashtrees, 47 Town Street, Duffield, Derbyshire, England.

Riding. Tower House, Southampton Street, London, England.

Useful Addresses

United States

American Horse Council
1700 K Street NW
Washington, D.C. 20006

American Horse Protection
Association
1312 18th Street NW
Washington, D.C. 20036

American Horse Shows Association
598 Madison Avenue
New York, New York 10022

Arabian Horse Club Registry
of America
120 South La Salle Street
Chicago, Illinois 60603

International Arabian Horse
Association
224 East Olive Avenue
Burbank, California
91502

National 4-H Council
7100 Connecticut Avenue
Chevy Chase, Maryland 20815

National Horse Show Association
of America
One Penn Plaza, Suite 4501
New York, New York 10119

National Steeplechase and
Hunt Association
Box 308
Elmont, New York 11003

Pony of the Americas Club, Inc.
P.O. Box 1447
Mason City, Iowa 50401

U.S. Combined Training Association
292 Bridge Street
South Hamilton, Maryland 01982

U.S. Dressage Federation
P.O. Box 80668
Lincoln, Nebraska 68501

U.S. Equestrian Team, Inc.
Gladstone, New Jersey 07934

U.S. Pony Clubs, Inc.
303 South High Street
West Chester, Pennsylvania 19380

U.S. Trotting Association
750 Michigan Avenue
Columbus, Ohio 43215

Canada

Alberta Equestrian Federation
7138 Fisher Street S.E.
Calgary, Alberta T2H 0W5

British Columbia Horse Owners'
Association
P.O. Box 131
Maple Ridge, British Columbia
V2X 7E9

Canadian Combined Training
Association
RR # 2
Caledon, Ontario L0N 1C0

Canadian Equestrian Federation
333 River Road
Ottawa, Ontario K1L 8H9

Canadian Equestrian Team
612 Sherbourne Street
Toronto, Ontario M4X 1L5

Canadian Horse and Pony Protection
Association
c/o Kimblewicks Acres
RR # 2
Lambeth, Ontario N0L 1S0

Canadian Pony Club Association
c/o Mr. Basil Kuglin
RR # 1
Foxboro, Ontario K0K 2B0

Canadian Pony Society
387 Hay Street
Woodstock, Ontario N4S 2C5

Canadian Trotting Association
233 Evans Avenue
Toronto, Ontario M8Z 1J6

Fédération equestre du Québec
1415 est, rue Jarry
Montreal, Quebec H2E 2Z7

Manitoba Horse Council
1700 Ellice Avenue
Winnipeg, Manitoba R3H 0B1

New Brunswick Equestrian
Association
691 Boulevard St. Pierre ouest
Caraquet, New Brunswick E0B 1K0

Nova Scotia Equestrian Federation
6340 Cornwall Street
Halifax, Nova Scotia B3H 2J1

Ontario Equestrian Federation
1220 Sheppard Avenue East
Willowdale, Ontario M2K 2X1

Trail Riders of the
Canadian Rockies
P.O. Box 6742, Station D
Calgary, Alberta T2P 2E6

Great Britain

British Driving Society
10 Marley Avenue
New Milton
Hampshire, England

British Field Sports Society
59 Kennington Road
London, England

British Horse Society
British Equestrian Centre
Kenilworth, Warwickshire
England

British Show Jumping Association
British Equestrian Centre
Kenilworth, Warwickshire
England

British Show Pony Society
The Croft House
East Road, Oundle
Peterborough, England

National Pony Society
7 Cross-and-Pillory Lane
Alton, Hampshire
England

The Pony Club
British Equestrian Centre
Kenilworth, Warwickshire
England

Calendar of Equestrian Events

January

Equestrian Alternatives, Newhall, California
Pegasus Dressage, Orlando, Florida

February

Almaden–U.S. Equestrian Team Palm Beach Classic, West Palm Beach, Florida
California Mid-Winter National, Los Angeles, California
Florida State Fair, Tampa, Florida
Insilco Masters of Palm Beach, West Palm Beach, Florida

March

American Invitational, Tampa, Florida
Dortmund International Horse Show, Dortmund, West Germany

April

Badminton Horse Trials, England
Royal Manitoba Winter Fair, Brandon, Manitoba

May

Bloomfield Open Hunt Spring Dressage, Bloomfield Hills, Michigan
Bloomfield Open Hunt Spring Hunter/Jumper, Bloomfield Hills, Michigan
Calgary International Horse Show, Calgary, Alberta
Rome Horse Show, Rome, Italy
U.S. Open Jumping Championship, Charlotte, North Carolina

June

Canadian Pony Breeders Show, King City, Ontario
Detroit Hunter/Jumper, Bloomfield Hills, Michigan
Devon Horse Show (Jumper), Devon, Pennsylvania
Dressage and Jumping Derby, Hamburg, West Germany
Epsom Derby, England
European Championships
Grand Prix de Paris, Longchamps, France
International Equestrian Organization Dressage, York, Pennsylvania
Lake Placid, Lake Placid, New York
Los Angeles Grand Prix and Jumping Classic, Los Angeles, California
North American Grand Prix
Rolex Kentucky Horse Trials, Lexington, Kentucky
Spruce Meadows National, Calgary, Alberta
U.S. Olympic Committee National Sports Festival, Colorado Springs, Colorado

July

Dressage at Devon, Devon, Pennsylvania
Dressagefest, Mason, Michigan
Hickstead Derby, Hickstead, England
Spruce Meadows Junior, Calgary, Alberta
White City Horse Show, London, England

August

Aachen Horse Show, Aachen, West Germany
American Continental Young Riders Championships, Hamilton, Maryland
Canadian National Exhibition, Toronto, Ontario
Cheltenham Gold Cup Horse Show, Oakville, Ontario
Dublin Horse Show, Dublin, Ireland
Eastern U.S. Dressage Championships
Jumping and Dressage Competition, Rotterdam, Netherlands
Ohio Dressage Derby, Cleveland, Ohio
Pan-American Games, 1983, Venezuela

September

All American Horse Classic, Indianapolis, Indiana
American Gold Cup, Devon, Pennsylvania
International Jumping Derby, Portsmouth, Rhode Island
Los Angeles International Jumping Festival, Los Angeles, California
Northwest International Horse Show, Vancouver, British Columbia
Olympics 1984, Los Angeles, California
Spruce Meadows Masters, Calgary, Alberta

October

Arc de Triomphe, Longchamps, France
Atlantic Winter Fair, Halifax, Nova Scotia
Canadian Dressage Championships, Toronto, Ontario
Dunhill Grand Prix, Toronto, Ontario
Horse of the Year Show, London, England
U.S. Dressage Championships (Insilco Cup)
U.S. Equestrian Team Medal Finals East, Gladstone, New Jersey

November

National Horse Show, New York City
Royal Agricultural Winter Fair, Toronto, Ontario

1983

JANUARY							FEBRUARY							MARCH						
S	M	T	W	T	F	S	S	M	T	W	T	F	S	S	M	T	W	T	F	S
						1			1	2	3	4	5			1	2	3	4	5
2	3	4	5	6	7	8	6	7	8	9	10	11	12	6	7	8	9	10	11	12
9	10	11	12	13	14	15	13	14	15	16	17	18	19	13	14	15	16	17	18	19
16	17	18	19	20	21	22	20	21	22	23	24	25	26	20	21	22	23	24	25	26
23	24	25	26	27	28	29	27	28						27	28	29	30	31		
30	31																			

APRIL							MAY							JUNE						
S	M	T	W	T	F	S	S	M	T	W	T	F	S	S	M	T	W	T	F	S
					1	2	1	2	3	4	5	6	7				1	2	3	4
3	4	5	6	7	8	9	8	9	10	11	12	13	14	5	6	7	8	9	10	11
10	11	12	13	14	15	16	15	16	17	18	19	20	21	12	13	14	15	16	17	18
17	18	19	20	21	22	23	22	23	24	25	26	27	28	19	20	21	22	23	24	25
24	25	26	27	28	29	30	29	30	31					26	27	28	29	30		

JULY							AUGUST							SEPTEMBER						
S	M	T	W	T	F	S	S	M	T	W	T	F	S	S	M	T	W	T	F	S
					1	2		1	2	3	4	5	6					1	2	3
3	4	5	6	7	8	9	7	8	9	10	11	12	13	4	5	6	7	8	9	10
10	11	12	13	14	15	16	14	15	16	17	18	19	20	11	12	13	14	15	16	17
17	18	19	20	21	22	23	21	22	23	24	25	26	27	18	19	20	21	22	23	24
24	25	26	27	28	29	30	28	29	30	31				25	26	27	28	29	30	
31																				

OCTOBER							NOVEMBER							DECEMBER						
S	M	T	W	T	F	S	S	M	T	W	T	F	S	S	M	T	W	T	F	S
						1			1	2	3	4	5					1	2	3
2	3	4	5	6	7	8	6	7	8	9	10	11	12	4	5	6	7	8	9	10
9	10	11	12	13	14	15	13	14	15	16	17	18	19	11	12	13	14	15	16	17
16	17	18	19	20	21	22	20	21	22	23	24	25	26	18	19	20	21	22	23	24
23	24	25	26	27	28	29	27	28	29	30				25	26	27	28	29	30	31
30	31																			

1984

JANUARY							FEBRUARY							MARCH						
S	M	T	W	T	F	S	S	M	T	W	T	F	S	S	M	T	W	T	F	S
1	2	3	4	5	6	7			1	2	3	4						1	2	3
8	9	10	11	12	13	14	5	6	7	8	9	10	11	4	5	6	7	8	9	10
15	16	17	18	19	20	21	12	13	14	15	16	17	18	11	12	13	14	15	16	17
22	23	24	25	26	27	28	19	20	21	22	23	24	25	18	19	20	21	22	23	24
29	30	31					26	27	28	29				25	26	27	28	29	30	31

APRIL							MAY							JUNE						
S	M	T	W	T	F	S	S	M	T	W	T	F	S	S	M	T	W	T	F	S
1	2	3	4	5	6	7			1	2	3	4	5						1	2
8	9	10	11	12	13	14	6	7	8	9	10	11	12	3	4	5	6	7	8	9
15	16	17	18	19	20	21	13	14	15	16	17	18	19	10	11	12	13	14	15	16
22	23	24	25	26	27	28	20	21	22	23	24	25	26	17	18	19	20	21	22	23
29	30						27	28	29	30	31			24	25	26	27	28	29	30

JULY							AUGUST							SEPTEMBER						
S	M	T	W	T	F	S	S	M	T	W	T	F	S	S	M	T	W	T	F	S
1	2	3	4	5	6	7				1	2	3	4							1
8	9	10	11	12	13	14	5	6	7	8	9	10	11	2	3	4	5	6	7	8
15	16	17	18	19	20	21	12	13	14	15	16	17	18	9	10	11	12	13	14	15
22	23	24	25	26	27	28	19	20	21	22	23	24	25	16	17	18	19	20	21	22
29	30	31					26	27	28	29	30	31		23	24	25	26	27	28	29
														30						

OCTOBER							NOVEMBER							DECEMBER						
S	M	T	W	T	F	S	S	M	T	W	T	F	S	S	M	T	W	T	F	S
	1	2	3	4	5	6					1	2	3							1
7	8	9	10	11	12	13	4	5	6	7	8	9	10	2	3	4	5	6	7	8
14	15	16	17	18	19	20	11	12	13	14	15	16	17	9	10	11	12	13	14	15
21	22	23	24	25	26	27	18	19	20	21	22	23	24	16	17	18	19	20	21	22
28	29	30	31				25	26	27	28	29	30		23	24	25	26	27	28	29
														30	31					

1985

JANUARY
S	M	T	W	T	F	S
		1	2	3	4	5
6	7	8	9	10	11	12
13	14	15	16	17	18	19
20	21	22	23	24	25	26
27	28	29	30	31		

FEBRUARY
S	M	T	W	T	F	S
					1	2
3	4	5	6	7	8	9
10	11	12	13	14	15	16
17	18	19	20	21	22	23
24	25	26	27	28		

MARCH
S	M	T	W	T	F	S
					1	2
3	4	5	6	7	8	9
10	11	12	13	14	15	16
17	18	19	20	21	22	23
24	25	26	27	28	29	30
31						

APRIL
S	M	T	W	T	F	S
	1	2	3	4	5	6
7	8	9	10	11	12	13
14	15	16	17	18	19	20
21	22	23	24	25	26	27
28	29	30				

MAY
S	M	T	W	T	F	S
			1	2	3	4
5	6	7	8	9	10	11
12	13	14	15	16	17	18
19	20	21	22	23	24	25
26	27	28	29	30	31	

JUNE
S	M	T	W	T	F	S
						1
2	3	4	5	6	7	8
9	10	11	12	13	14	15
16	17	18	19	20	21	22
23	24	25	26	27	28	29
30						

JULY
S	M	T	W	T	F	S
	1	2	3	4	5	6
7	8	9	10	11	12	13
14	15	16	17	18	19	20
21	22	23	24	25	26	27
28	29	30	31			

AUGUST
S	M	T	W	T	F	S
				1	2	3
4	5	6	7	8	9	10
11	12	13	14	15	16	17
18	19	20	21	22	23	24
25	26	27	28	29	30	31

SEPTEMBER
S	M	T	W	T	F	S
1	2	3	4	5	6	7
8	9	10	11	12	13	14
15	16	17	18	19	20	21
22	23	24	25	26	27	28
29	30					

OCTOBER
S	M	T	W	T	F	S
		1	2	3	4	5
6	7	8	9	10	11	12
13	14	15	16	17	18	19
20	21	22	23	24	25	26
27	28	29	30	31		

NOVEMBER
S	M	T	W	T	F	S
					1	2
3	4	5	6	7	8	9
10	11	12	13	14	15	16
17	18	19	20	21	22	23
24	25	26	27	28	29	30

DECEMBER
S	M	T	W	T	F	S
1	2	3	4	5	6	7
8	9	10	11	12	13	14
15	16	17	18	19	20	21
22	23	24	25	26	27	28
29	30	31				

1986

JANUARY
S	M	T	W	T	F	S
			1	2	3	4
5	6	7	8	9	10	11
12	13	14	15	16	17	18
19	20	21	22	23	24	25
26	27	28	29	30	31	

FEBRUARY
S	M	T	W	T	F	S
						1
2	3	4	5	6	7	8
9	10	11	12	13	14	15
16	17	18	19	20	21	22
23	24	25	26	27	28	

MARCH
S	M	T	W	T	F	S
						1
2	3	4	5	6	7	8
9	10	11	12	13	14	15
16	17	18	19	20	21	22
23	24	25	26	27	28	29
30	31					

APRIL
S	M	T	W	T	F	S
		1	2	3	4	5
6	7	8	9	10	11	12
13	14	15	16	17	18	19
20	21	22	23	24	25	26
27	28	29	30			

MAY
S	M	T	W	T	F	S
				1	2	3
4	5	6	7	8	9	10
11	12	13	14	15	16	17
18	19	20	21	22	23	24
25	26	27	28	29	30	31

JUNE
S	M	T	W	T	F	S
1	2	3	4	5	6	7
8	9	10	11	12	13	14
15	16	17	18	19	20	21
22	23	24	25	26	27	28
29	30					

JULY
S	M	T	W	T	F	S
		1	2	3	4	5
6	7	8	9	10	11	12
13	14	15	16	17	18	19
20	21	22	23	24	25	26
27	28	29	30	31		

AUGUST
S	M	T	W	T	F	S
					1	2
3	4	5	6	7	8	9
10	11	12	13	14	15	16
17	18	19	20	21	22	23
24	25	26	27	28	29	30
31						

SEPTEMBER
S	M	T	W	T	F	S
	1	2	3	4	5	6
7	8	9	10	11	12	13
14	15	16	17	18	19	20
21	22	23	24	25	26	27
28	29	30				

OCTOBER
S	M	T	W	T	F	S
			1	2	3	4
5	6	7	8	9	10	11
12	13	14	15	16	17	18
19	20	21	22	23	24	25
26	27	28	29	30	31	

NOVEMBER
S	M	T	W	T	F	S
						1
2	3	4	5	6	7	8
9	10	11	12	13	14	15
16	17	18	19	20	21	22
23	24	25	26	27	28	29
30						

DECEMBER
S	M	T	W	T	F	S
	1	2	3	4	5	6
7	8	9	10	11	12	13
14	15	16	17	18	19	20
21	22	23	24	25	26	27
28	29	30	31			

About the author:
Christilot Hanson Boylen was born in Indonesia and came to Canada with her parents when she was four years old. Her mother, Willy Blok Hanson, was a well-known dance instructor, and Chris began dancing professionally at an early age. But she always wanted to ride and work with horses.

When she was ten, her parents finally allowed her to buy a horse and join the Toronto Pony Club. Chris became involved with three-day eventing and eventually found herself specializing in dressage. At seventeen she became the youngest person to compete in the Grand Prix de Dressage event at the Tokyo Olympics.

In 1971 Chris won the individual gold medal in dressage at the Pan-American Games, as well as the Coupe Carven at the prestigious Aachen Horse Show where she was the leading female dressage rider. In 1975 she again won the gold medal at the Pan-American Games and in 1976 she finished sixth in the Grand Prix de Dressage at the Montreal Olympics. She has been Canadian Dressage Champion nine times.

Chris Boylen is the founder of the Canadian Dressage Owners and Riders Association. She was named Horsewoman of the Year by the National Equestrian Federation of Canada in 1970 and 1971, and is the author of *Canadian Entry*, her autobiography, and *Basic Dressage for North America*. She has two daughters, Billie Jeanne and Christa-Dora, and lives near the International Equestrian Sports Centre outside Toronto.

About the illustrator:
Elaine Macpherson is a prominent Canadian illustrator who has been sketching horses since she drew her first horse ("brown, with red legs and a purple mane and tail") at the age of four. She polished her craft by sketching the horses that she saw on the television westerns, and began riding at the age of five. When she was 12 she won first prize at her first gymkhana and first prize in a drawing contest. She attended Saturday-morning art classes at the Art Gallery of Ontario until the age of 18 and graduated from the Ontario College of Art a few years later. She now has her own art studio where she does work for riding stores, jockey clubs, trotting associations and equestrian publications. Over the years she has competed in several equitation and dressage competitions. Her horse, "Shad," is a five-year-old bay Thoroughbred.

Acknowledgments

The publisher would like to thank the following for permission to reproduce copyrighted material:

Page 10: J.B. Lippincott Co. for *The Green Grass of Wyoming* by Mary O'Hara, copyright 1946, copyright renewed 1974 by Mary O'Hara; page 22: Jonathan Cape for *No Ponies* by Mary Treadgold, illustrated by Ruth Gervis, copyright © 1981; page 24: E.P. Dutton Inc. for *Runaway Stallion* by Walt Morey, copyright © 1973 by Walt Morey; page 36: Copyright © 1978 from the book *The Girl Who Loved Wild Horses* by Paul Goble. Reprinted with permission of Bradbury Press, Inc. Scarsdale, NY 10583; pages 38 and 50: from *Flambards in Summer/Fly-by-Night* by K.M. Peyton, published by Oxford University Press © K.M. Peyton; page 62: E.P. Dutton Inc. for *Year of the Black Pony* by Walt Morey, copyright © 1976 by Walt Morey; page 74: *The Black Stallion* by Walter Farley, copyright 1941 by Walter Farley, copyright renewed 1969 by Walter Farley, published by Random House, Inc.; page 76: Delacorte Press for *The Horseman's Word* by Georgess McHargue, copyright © 1981 by Georgess McHargue; page 88: from *The Year of the Horse* by Diana Walker (Abelard-Schuman). Copyright © 1975 by Diana Walker. Reprinted by permission of Harper & Row, Publishers, Inc.; page 90: George Allen & Unwin and Houghton Mifflin for *Lord of the Rings* by J.R.R. Tolkien, copyright 1954; page 100: From *National Velvet* by Enid Bagnold, illustrated by Laurian Jones, copyright 1935 by Enid Bagnold, copyright renewed 1963 by Enid Bagnold Jones. Reprinted by permission of Brandt & Brandt Literary Agents, Inc.; page 102: *The Black Stallion* by Walter Farley, copyright 1941 by Walter Farley, copyright renewed 1969 by Walter Farley, published by Random House, Inc.; page 108: Grosset & Dunlap for illustration from *Gulliver's Travels* by Jonathan Swift, illustrated by Aldren Watson, copyright 1947; page 112: The extract and illustration from *Sun Horse, Moon Horse* by Rosemary Sutcliff and illustrated by Shirley Felts is reproduced by permission of The Bodley Head and Murray Pollinger Ltd.; page 126: From *Misty of Chincoteague* by Marguerite Henry. Illustration by Wesley Dennis. © 1947, 1975 Rand McNally & Company; page 138: Clarke, Irwin & Company for *Canadian Entry* by Christilot Hanson Boylen, copyright © 1966; page 140: From *The Catch Colt* by Mary O'Hara, used by permission of the Canadian Publishers, McClelland and Stewart Limited, Toronto; page 154: From *National Velvet* by Enid Bagnold, illustrated by Laurian Jones, copyright 1935 by Enid Bagnold, copyright renewed 1963 by Enid Bagnold Jones. Reprinted by permission of Brandt & Brandt Literary Agents, Inc.

Photo credits
Pages 8, 20, 34, 48, 60, 72, 80, 86, 98, 110, 124, 136,150,174 and back cover: Birgitte Nielsen; page 16: Wilkinson Photography; page 30: Waintrob-Budd; page 42: Elizabeth Millar; page 56: Equus Studios; page 106: Wolfgang Eckhardt; page 118: Debby Jamroz; page 130: Paul Macpherson; pages 132 and 146: Czerny; page 158: Rock Eden Farm.

The next edition . . .

Now that you've used this diary, I'd like to know what you think of it—what you like best about the book, what you'd like to see changed, added or left out. What features would you like to see in a future edition? Perhaps you have a suggestion for an interesting bit of trivia that you've discovered, or a quote from your favorite horse story.

Send us your comments, and if we use your suggestion in the next edition of *The Horse-Lover's Diary*, you'll receive a free copy of the book. Fill out this page and send it to me, Christilot Hanson Boylen, c/o Madison Press Books, 149 Lowther Avenue, Toronto, Ontario, Canada M5R 3M5.

The best thing about *The Horse-Lover's Diary* is:

I would like to see more information on the following topics:

My favorite horse book:

My horse tip/trivia:

Other Comments:

Name:

Address:

Did you   receive *The Horse-Lover's Diary* as a gift? _____

           buy *The Horse-Lover's Diary* yourself? _____